A Concise History of Modern Architecture in India

Light and Shade, The British Council Building, New Delhi

A Concise History of Modern Architecture in India

JON LANG

permanent black

Published by
PERMANENT BLACK
'Himalayana', Mall Road, Ranikhet Cantt,
Ranikhet 263645
Email: perblack@gmail.com

Distributed by
ORIENT BLACKSWAN PRIVATE LIMITED
Bangalore Bhopal Bhubaneshwar Chandigarh Chennai
Ernakulam Guwahati Hyderabad Jaipur Kolkata
Lucknow Mumbai New Delhi Patna
www.orientblackswan.com

First published in hardback 2002

First Paperback printing 2010
Third Impression 2018
ISBN 81-7824-305-9

Printed and bound by Sapra Brothers, New Delhi 110092

Contents

Preface

INDIA HAS an extraordinarily rich architectural history and a great variety of current professional practices. Understanding them enriches the study of architecture everywhere. This book has the advantage of offering a disinterested view of architecture in India as it is allied neither with a school of architectural thought nor some aspect of the politics of the profession and professional attitudes in the country—perhaps partly because it is by a foreigner. It has, however, been written within a particular intellectual tradition, especially in its division of architectural philosophies into two broad categories: Rationalist and Empiricist. And while I am critical of much Modernist and Post-Modernist architecture I believe that 'the Modernists almost got it right' and recognise that all buildings are designed within an economic and political context. Above all it is as a non-historian with a social science rather than a humanities orientation to architectural theory that I have written. Like others then this history is an offering to debate, in this instance, on the nature of architecture and its role in society.

The book has been written with Indian architectural students in mind and focuses on describing the variety of ideas shaping architecture in India. It is hoped that it will be of interest to the practising architect too. The goal has been to present an intellectual overview of the various sub-plots within the history of architecture in India and to introduce some of the players. It is a concise view of a complex history. No single book can capture India's diversity of architectural works and architects. Some buildings have been chosen, often arbitrarily, to represent lines of thinking and others, equally important, have been neglected. There are many fine architects and architectural firms whose work is not represented here. Indeed, the book focuses not on architects but on lines of architectural thought. As a result, few of the architects mentioned in the text will find what they regard as their best, or even most representative work, described in the book.

Many readers, particularly young students for whom the past may seem to be one long blur, will be dismayed by the number of dates in the book. The dates are important for they show when architectural ideas were being explored and at what point in the architects' careers. They also enable fairly accurate inferences to be made about the potential influences of the work of one architect on that of another. *All* architects of the modern era have been inspired by earlier architects, borrowing ideas from them and then, often without acknowledgment, making them their own (Williamson, 1991). Although many architects present themselves to the world as born geniuses, it is clearly not so. Le Corbusier, one of the twentieth century's architectural giants, for instance, took ideas from the past and from his colleagues with little acknowledgment and often misled others about his own background and education to enhance his self-image (Brooks, 1997). Indian architects owe much to other architects and to the world around them as indeed the world to Indian architects. This book is as much about the flow of ideas as about architects and buildings.

The goal of this book has been neither to praise Indian architecture nor Indian architects although there is much praiseworthy work and many highly creative architects. Laudatory texts abound. Those seeking a fine arts text, or an '*architalk*' book, will be disappointed. Here I seek to describe and explain architectural norms as they have been shaped in the country. It is the understanding of these processes that enhances the development of architectural theory. If this book proves to be a base from which scholars, individually or collectively, can delve more deeply into modern Indian architectural histories, it will have served its purpose.

JON LANG

Sydney
October 2000

The LIC Building, Chennai

1

Modernism and Modern Architecture

MODERN SIMPLY means up-to-date. The term also attributes certain characteristics to a person or society. One of the hallmarks of a modern society is division of labour. The very existence of a profession in which the design of a product is separated from its making is one such division. In architecture there have been people who have specialised in designing buildings since the beginning of recorded history. Until recently, however, they also played an integrated role in the construction of a project. In India, the bulk of building design and construction is still in the hands of the *mistri* or contractor who both designs and builds. Architects have however played an increasingly significant role in society, in particular, developing conceptions and reflections of modern life in built form.

Perceptions of what constitutes being modern, up-to-date, in architecture vary. In this book, Classical Architecture and the Neo-Classical are not regarded as modern but architects whose *oeuvre* today relies heavily on the Classical, take the position that Classical Architecture is always modern because it resonates psychologically and physiologically with the human spirit. A 1950s guidebook to post-Independence Calcutta refers to Neo-Classical architecture as modern because it was the predominant style of contemporary architectural practice (Barry, 1954). However, by the 1940s, in Calcutta itself, some of what were regarded as India's first International Modernist buildings had already been built. Edgar Tafel, later an apprentice for Frank Lloyd Wright, writing about the modern architecture of Calcutta in the 1940s would certainly have regarded the Neo-Classical not as modern but as old-fashioned (Tafel, 1945). A highly Modernist building, the Garden Theatre and Lighthouse Cinema in Calcutta (1936–8), designed by the Dutch architect Willem Marinus Dudok (1884–1974), was fully operative by then.

In everyday usage, the word 'modern' does imply a departure from the norm, from usual practice. In the history of architecture there have been a number of movements that have referred to themselves as Modern. So too in India. Sometimes these groups have been contemporaries but each has presented a very different view of what being up-to-date means. During the 1930s in India, Art Deco, International Modernism and the Modern Indian Architecture Movement were all referred to by their protagonists as modern. The first two were certainly presenting a new face to the world, but the third sought an up-to-dateness in the past. It was a revivalist movement. All three had legitimate claims to being modern; each sought to make an expression, in architectural form, of modern times, of being the most appropriate for India. So what then is modernism?

MODERNISM

Modernism is an attitude. An attitude is composed of a belief and a value. A modernist is someone who believes that there are better ways of doing things. A modernist is also someone whose whole line of thinking owes much to the spirit of the enlightenment—to the belief that the world can be improved—that it can and should be made a better place for better people. India has a rich history of modernist thinkers and doers from Raja Rammohan Roy (1772–1833) to Rabindranath Tagore (1861–1941) to Jawarharlal Nehru (1889–1964). Certainly, the euphoria that followed independence in 1947 fired the hearts and minds of architects about what India could and should be.

Westernisation is often considered a synonym for modernisation, and certainly, many ideas from the West have flowed into India. This observation holds particularly for technologies developed during the past two centuries. It also holds for the nature of the architectural profession itself. Nevertheless, one should be cautious about the generalisations one makes because at the same time, ideas from India have influenced the West, often in subtle ways. In the late nineteenth century, the architectural battles in India both reflected and contributed to the international debate. The writings of James Fergusson (1808–86) on Indian architecture fuelled the discussion on architecture in London. Again, in the 1970s and 1980s, to a large extent, it was the experience in India of Modernist architecture that reshaped the thinking about it throughout the world (e.g., Brolin, 1976). However, the potential contribution of an understanding of architecture in India to architectural theory is largely ignored.

In architecture, a modernist is often considered to be somebody who simply supports any break with the past. Often it is a person who advocates a new look for buildings—a new style. Architects may be more concerned with the spatial organisation of buildings—the way spaces are enclosed and related to each other, their composition geometrically and/or in their sequence as an observer moves through them. More broadly, a modernist architect believes that architecture is a medium for improving the lives of people.

What has to be avoided when thinking in this manner is the belief that the built environment can determine people's behaviour. The built environment can only provide behavioural and aesthetic *affordances*, or opportunities. That reality can, nevertheless, be a powerful contributor to the way people shape the qualities of their lives. The difficulty is that Modernist architecture is also, despite many protestations to the contrary, a set of styles; ways of solving problems using particular sets of patterns.

To have a new architecture one not only needs designers who think in new ways but clients who seek departures from the past. The clients for modern architecture throughout the world have been people making financial or intellectual progress in society or attempting to do so (Eaton, 1969). In Ahmedabad, for instance, it was the mill-owning families. They were people breaking from traditions partly because new technologies were available to be exploited but also to break what they perceived to be the shackles of the social norms of their own cultures.

We live in an age of rapid change when being up-to-date is very important to many people. The fashion industry thrives on such human desires. In wholeheartedly seeking change in order to be modern there is the danger of throwing out the good with the bad. Much can be learnt from the past. Modern architecture, and what we accept as being modern, has been shaped by the debate between those who design buildings based on methods proven successful in the past and those who seek something completely fresh based on a perception of brave new worlds.

EMPIRICISM AND RATIONALISM IN ARCHITECTURE

Any concise history of complex ideas runs the danger of presenting a caricature of those ideas because it exaggerates points of view in order to encapsulate positions. Each philosophical approach to studying architecture represents a way of looking at the world and of setting out to change it. In Western philosophy, at least, there have been two very different approaches to thinking about how best to shape the future: *Empiricism* and *Rationalism.* Empiricists argue that knowledge should be based on evidence. Rationalists argue that truth and beauty can be divined by pure reasoning. These two modes of thought are powerful and pervasive. They explain much about architecture but, like any classification system, they can also place blinkers on the way we look at the world around us.

Architectural movements and architects too can be classified as Empiricist or Rationalist although individual architects may have switched from one mode of thinking to the other during their careers, indeed in addressing different contemporary problems. Such an observation can be made about the leading luminaries of the Indian architectural scene over the past fifty years: Charles Correa, B.V. Doshi and Achyut Kanvinde. In reality, almost all architectural thinking straddles the two philosophical approaches to some extent. It must not be thought for a moment that there was no empirical reality to Rationalist thought any more than that there was no rationalism behind empirical design ideologies. Both Empiricists and Rationalists have drawn conclusions from the same world. What distinguishes the two is that Rationalists have been willing to stick their necks out about the future based on personal beliefs about the world while Empiricists have been more conservative, believing that it is essential to base approaches to design on careful observations of the present. Empiricists, nevertheless, use considerable logical speculation in their work and, if one scratches the surface, Rationalists rely on precedents to a much greater extent than they are usually willing to admit. They fear they will seem to be less creative if their architectural ideas are not seen to be complete inventions.

The architectural *avant-gardes*, particularly those who see themselves as pure fine artists, have generally held Rationalists in high esteem because they break with the past. In thinking about modern architecture it is often only the Rationalist approach that is considered legitimately modern. This attitude is partly due to the visual novelty of Rationalists' building forms and partly because Rationalism was seen to be tied to radical (i.e., socialist) political orientations. Many Empiricists too, however, while drawing from their perceptions of what already works, have broken new ground and have had similar political attitudes. They have, however, thought about the future in a different way.

Empiricists have relied on precedents. These precedents vary from historical patterns or styles of architectural form, to patterns that seem to be fulfilling the needs of contemporary lives. Over the last four decades there has been a significant shift in Empiricist thought. There has been a much greater reliance on an approach to design based not on precedents but on abstract theory derived from systematic research. Architecture is seen more as an applied behavioural science than as a pure fine art (Rapoport, 1977; Lang, 1987). The avant-garde insist on the opposite and paradoxically, become the intellectual conservatives!

In India, the architectural Empiricists can be divided into four sub-groups. They are: 1) the Revivalists—those who simply copy the present or past; 2) those who use precedents in a highly innovative manner; 3) the Post-Modernists—those who abstract elements of the past to use symbolically in new buildings, and potentially 4) the applied behavioural scientists—those who look for lessons in the way the environment functions. Their common goal has been to create humane buildings that deal with life as it is lived rather than buildings based on some vision of the way life should be. Sometimes this approach has been called 'Humanist' but the label should be used with caution. One should be equally cautious about applying the adjectives 'Romantic' or 'Picturesque' to it. The story is more complex than any of these terms suggest.

Internationally, twentieth century Rationalist architects consisted of a more diverse set of people than the Empiricists because they were dealing not with actual models of buildings and nature but futures and geometries that they imagined. As a result new social ideas as well as new massing ideas were explored; the latter were based primarily on the pure forms of cubes and cylinders. There were thus an open-ended number of architectural possibilities constrained only by technological reality. In India, Rationalist architecture has been more narrowly focused than in the rest of the world because of the power of two major influences—first the work of the Bauhaus architects of the 1920s and 1930s and then later, during the 1950s, that of Le Corbusier. Much Rationalist architecture in the country as a consequence owes more to the forms of the Bauhaus and Le Corbusier than the spirit of Rationalist thought.

The history of modern architecture—i.e., up-to-date architecture—in India shows that there have been shifts back and forth between Empiricist and Rationalist attitudes. Often the two ideological approaches competed for supremacy both in architectural practice and in architectural education. The spirit of Independence at mid-century sparked much Rationalist thinking about what the new architecture of India should be. The experiences with buildings and urban designs so generated have tilted the balance in the Empiricist direction.

One of the radical new precepts of the twentieth century in countries like India was that of the architect as individual artistic creator and the consideration of buildings as works of art that were serving the more mundane purposes of everyday life. The design process has become much more self-conscious and professional bodies have appeared to promote (and control) the creation of products by their members. In Europe and North America, these bodies have a history dating back to the middle of the nineteenth century. The Indian Institute of Architects has only been in existence since the 1920s—a date that coincides with the final successful political drive for a new country and for a new architecture to go with it. It is also the date at which this history begins.

Since the 1920s, different clients have sought different types of architecture based on who they themselves were or, more frequently perhaps, desired to be. The clients for Empiricist architecture have historically been people of very different backgrounds from those who sought Rationalist designs. Those seeking Empiricist Modernism tended to be self-made manufacturers and entrepreneurs; those seeking Rationalist architecture were more closely allied with ground-breaking political and fine art movements. For much of the century, Rationalist architects were also able to capture the attention and support of many highly significant governmental leaders and officials, Jawaharlal Nehru amongst them. Those seeking Revivalist architecture or the maintenance of traditions were, and still tend to be, from families who have long been leaders in their own social worlds. The modern Empiricists fell in between the two groups.

The twentieth century saw an extraordinary array of architectural explorations. Most of the ideas that are with us now were developed during the first half of the century when the world was turned upside down as a result of technological, social and political changes. The changes came more slowly in the second half of the century. We can learn much from the successes and failures of Modernist and post-Modernist architectural thought as different people within different cultural contexts perceive them. This story deals with the Indian experience.

Galconde, Pondicherry

2

Early Modern Architecture in India: 1920 to 1950

THE THREE decades between 1920 and 1950 were a period of political ferment in India as the country painfully but inevitably made its way to political independence. So too in architecture as several streams of thought strove for professional hegemony. The newly-established Indian Institute of Architects was dominated by British-trained architects; many of the major architectural firms in the country were run by British and other foreign architects some of whom had spent their whole lives in India.

In Europe, neo-Classicism, the Art Deco, and Modernist architectural thought were vying for attention. (Modernist in this context refers to the groups who called themselves Modernist.) In the United States, the work of Frank Lloyd Wright was influential amongst architects but the work of the European Modernists considerably less so. The Philadelphia Saving Fund Society building, the first major Modernist office building in the country dates only from the middle of that decade. In India, the architectural work was either Neo-Classical, or some modified version of it, or Art Deco.

Architects in India were aware of the ferment in the European art and architectural worlds of the first three decades of the century. They knew of the work of the City Beautiful proponents (the construction of New Delhi was well under way), the proposals of the Bauhaus, the writings of Le Corbusier in Europe and the work of Frank Lloyd Wright in the United States and Japan. It was not, however, until well after Independence that the new ideas were absorbed into architectural practices and even then it was only a relatively small number of firms that actually embraced them.

By 1930, the art and architectural ideas of the swadeshi era had largely run their course although their impact on country towns and villages continued through to the 1950s. The allied architectural explorations of Surendranath Kar (1892–1970) in nationalist design at Shantiniketan, much inspired and directed by Rabindranath Tagore, had failed to capture the attention of the major architectural firms. Modernist art had already been displayed in Calcutta in a Bauhaus art exhibition showing the work of such international luminaries as Wassily Kandinsky (1866–1944) and Paul Klee (1879–1940). This exhibition was more influential in the world of fine arts than in architecture (Mitter, 1994; Lang, Desai and Desai, 1997). Although knowledgeable about alternative design ideologies internationally, the architectural discussion in India was locally centred.

Mumbai was the heart of architectural thinking in India during the period between the two World Wars. The major British-headed architectural firms as well as the newer Indian practices, were located there. Their evolution was parallel although by the mid-1930s the distinction between them in terms of personnel or the work they produced was increasingly blurred. The former, as the result of both political pressure and financial exigency, were taking on Indian partners who actually executed much of their work and the latter were essentially British-educated. The Sir J.J. School was the only significant place for architectural education in the country at the time and its teachers, such as Claude Batley (1879–1956), exerted an influence that has well outlasted their lifetimes. They argued for a gradual modernisation of architecture and certainly for any development to be cognisant of its Indian context.

A modified Classicism that hinted at the influence of International Modernism can be seen in some of the works of the major Mumbai firm of Gregson, Batley and King. Much of it, as in the Bank of India building (1944) in Mumbai, remained tied to the past. Their design for the Ahmedabad Town Hall (1938), however, despite classical overtones in its massing, has a simplicity in form and exposed masonry work that were new. The use of chhajjas and brackets reflects Batley's search for a new Indian architecture. The building, however, displays no new spatial order.

The designs of the buildings in the Ballard Estate, the first comprehensively planned precinct in Mumbai (1908–1923), owe much to Sir Edwin Lutyens (1869–1944) and his work in New Delhi. Neo-Classical work can, however, best be exemplified by buildings such as the Statesman Building in Calcutta (1931–3) and the buildings of the late 1930s and early 1940s—Dare House, Chennai House and the United Life Insurance Building (now Life Insurance Corporation of India Building)—all along N.S.C. Bose Road in Chennai. The work of the Calcutta firm of Sudlow, Ballardie and Thompson (later Ballardie, Thompson and Matthews) in buildings such as Virginia House, Calcutta (1928) and, particularly, the Lady Dufferin Hospital (1937) shows an abandonment of the Neo-Classical idiom of their Statesman Building design in favour of simpler forms.

Against this architectural backdrop, two British architects who had come out to help Lutyens in the design of New Delhi produced buildings radically different from those of the major architectural practices. The two were Walter Sykes George (1881–1962) who made his life in India and Arthur Gordon Shoosmith (1888–1974) whose contact was considerably briefer. George's designs for St Thomas'

Virginia House, Calcutta

Ahmedabad Town Hall

St Stephen's College, Delhi

St Mortens Garrison Church, Delhi

Church (1929), and St Stephen's College, Delhi (1938) are far removed from the neo-Classical. The church is built of unadorned brick, and the college of brick with a stone base. The simplicity of their façades and their massing show a dramatic departure from the contemporaneous work in India. The same observation can be made more forcefully about Shoosmith's St Martin's Garrison Church (1928–31) in the Delhi Cantonment. It is difficult to see the precedents on which Shoosmith drew; perhaps it was European expressionism. George's later design for the Tuberculosis Association Building (1950–2) is closer to the Modernist idiom that has prevailed in much Indian architecture since Independence. It was not, however, until the Indian architects first came home from studying in the United States of America during the 1940s that such architecture established more than a toehold in India. The influence of the Art Deco was much more immediate.

ART DECO

The Art Deco grew out of the Art Noveau—known in England as the 'modern style'—which had much influenced avant-garde European architecture between 1890 and 1910. The Art Noveau was romantic, anti-historical and highly individualistic in nature. The buildings were sinuous, undulating, asymmetrical and full of decorative forms, either floral or geometric. The Maison du Peuple, in Brussels (1896–9) designed by Victor Horta (1861–1947) or, perhaps, the work of Antonio Gaudí y Cornet (1852–1926) in Barcelona exemplify this work. Norma Evenson, a renowned architectural historian, regards the Esplanade Mansions (1910) in Calcutta, designed by Martin and Co., as an example of Art Noveau architecture (Evenson, 1989). There is, however, little evidence that either the Art Noveau in

Esplanade Mansions, Calcutta

Reid House, Calcutta

Europe or Esplanade Mansions had a significant impact on what followed in India.

During the 1950s and 1960s Art Deco was disparaged by Modernists because of its apparent whimsical nature. It has, however, stood the test of time better than much subsequent work and is now often warmly, and perhaps wryly, evaluated. Art Deco was a style of rich surfaces, sensuous textures and flowing forms. Much of it incorporated luxurious materials: marble, ivory, ebony and other expensive woods, mother of pearl and semi-precious stones. Its forms were clearly influenced by the Futurists of Italy, who were enamoured with the new speed of movements afforded by the car and aeroplane; by the Cubists in France; by the ancient architecture of various cultures such as the Moors, Aztecs, Mayas and Assyrians, and by pre-Raphaelite art in Europe. The opening up of new communication-modes—radio, telephone, magazines and films—had a direct impact on the forms used in the interior decoration of ocean liners and thence on both the interiors and exteriors of buildings.

These new modes of communication were represented in built form (as in product design) in the form of 'streamlining'. Streamlining represented economy, efficiency and speed. Logical for cars, aeroplanes and trains, streamlining for aerodynamic purposes in buildings was considerably, if not totally, subservient to its aesthetic appeal. The sleek curved style in buildings became known as 'Streamlined Moderne' or simply 'Moderne'. Façades were often divided into tripartite symmetries, with the central plane emphasised. Once mingled with American influences, Art Deco's decorative features on buildings included lightening bolt zigzags that added an angularity to curved building forms. The portrayal of the human figure in murals evolved from the more languid Art Noveau forms to sultry, even erotic, poses reflecting the optimistic and often hedonistic aspirations of the middle-class of the 1920s.

Many Art Deco edifices were built in India during the decades of the 1930s and 1940s and continued to be built well into the 1960s, by which time it was regarded as *passe* in Europe. In a time of political upheaval as Indian nationalists agitated increasingly for independence, the Art Deco was too radical an art form to be acceptable to imperialists and too foreign to be acceptable to swaraja idealists. Nevertheless, to a number of wealthy clients and architects, particularly in Mumbai, Art Deco was *the* expression of modernism. In the hands of British firms, Art Deco was used in the restrained manner of Europe. The Indian-headed firms such as G.B. Mhatre, K.P. Daver, Doctor, Mhatre and Desai, and Merwanji Bana and Co. used it with considerable flamboyance. In the hands of the traditional mistris it was often even more radical, if cruder.

Examples of Art Deco work can be found in all the major cities of India. The Kasturi Building (1939) for *The Hindu* in Chennai was designed by Major H[arold] Fellowes Prynne of Jackson and Barker. The Electricity Building (1940–1) in Ahmedabad was the work of Gregson, Batley and King. Ballardie, Thompson and Matthews designed the Reid Building (1942) in Calcutta; the firm still occupies space in it. All kinds of buildings were built in the Art Deco. There were hotels (e.g., Hotel Dasaprakash in Chennai, the Ritz (1942) in Mumbai and the Ranthambhore Tiger Reserve Hostel, Parsee agiaries (eg., the Marine Lines Agiary in Mumbai designed in 1936 by Shahpoorjee N. Chandabhoy), a number of flats and houses and, above all, cinemas.

Art Deco houses and apartment buildings have flat roofs, curving windows and a variety of decorative motifs. Favoured decorative patterns included sunrays, lightening bursts, aeroplanes, and palm trees etched in glass or in metal work or as bas-reliefs. Bungalows used bold horizontal forms and pastel colours. In two- and three- storey houses, the stairwells became prominent and ship-like with cylindrical forms; verandahs became curved. Material such as terrazzo, glass brick, etched glass and plywood came into vogue; cast iron fell into disuse. The furniture too followed Art Deco patterns often more boldly than the buildings themselves.

The Mangaldas Mehta House designed by Master, Sathe and Bhuta on Salebhoy Karimji Barodawalla Marg in Mumbai is an L-shaped building with a simple plan. Continuous cantilevered sunshades that were edged in red gave it some style (Alff, 1991). The Das residence (1939), designed by Martin Burns & Co in Calcutta has a similar exterior appearance. Flats such as May-Fair House (1935–7) designed by Merwanji Bana and Co, and Carmichael Apartments (1937) designed by Hermasji J. Billimoria followed a like character in multi-level buildings. There are a number of such buildings located in the Malabar Hill and Cumballa Hill areas of Mumbai and farther out in suburbs such as Bandra. It is, however, the Back Bay (Churchgate) reclamation area in the city that is the most extensive example of the Art Deco in India.

As an area, Back Bay, although it is considerably tarnished now, rivals the display of hotels on Miami Beach in the United States as an Art Deco precinct. Along Netaji Subhas Road (Marine Drive) many of the buildings have by now been much altered but the Art Deco underpinning of their designs is still clear. The row of buildings opposite the Pope Paul Maidan (Oval Maidan), still retains most of the external features and hallmarks of the spirit of Art Deco although the colours of most of the façades have long since faded. Court View, Fair Lawn, Green Fields, Queens Court, Windsor House, Shiv Shanti Bhavan, Belvedere Court, Ivorine, and Sunshine line the street, their names a reminder of the late colonial era in which they were built.

Shiv Shanti Bhavan, designed by Rajabali Patel, is typical. It is a reinforced concrete building with a stucco façade decorated with 'chevrons, triangles and zigzag motifs' (Alff, 1991). Empress Court, designed by Gajanan B. Mahtre, is another, if better executed than most, example of the Art Deco. The staircase and entrance hall in particular are emphasised with details such as carefully crafted newel posts (Mhatre, 1937). At the northern end of this Art Deco row is the Eros Cinema.

Shiv Shanti Bhavan, Mumbai

May-Fair House Mumbai

The Back Bay Reclamation Area, Mumbai

The films of the 1930s offered cinemagoers a world of fantasy that few could afford. So did the picture-palaces. In Mumbai, the Eros, Regal, Liberty and Metro alone offered over 5000 seats in air-conditioned comfort to patrons. The Roxy, Metro and Elite in Calcutta were major Art Deco cinemas in that city while Ahmedabad boasted the Relief, Lucknow the Mayfair, and Patna the Hind. The Mumbai examples were, and sixty years later remain, the most dramatic. They operate today as enthusiastically as in the past.

The Regal (1930–4) in Bombay was designed by Charles Stephens, the Metro (opened in 1938) was designed by Ditchburn and Mistri and the boldest, the Eros, (1935–8) by Sohrabji K. Bhedwar. They have many features in common. Their sites were in prominent, highly visible locations. All were mixed-use urban buildings but their entertainment components were the most prominent both in terms

The Eros Cinema, Mumbai

of bulk and in aesthetic expression. Each stressed the vertical in design, each has back lit marquees and each was designed to be seen at night as much as during the day. Their interiors are grand, with spacious vestibules adorned with murals and other decorative features (Dwivedi and Mehrotra, 1995).

Not a fantasy but a reality is Morvi Palace (1931–44) designed by Kumar Ramsinh (d.1956), a graduate of London's Architectural Association and the second Indian partner in Gregson Batley and King (P.A. d'Avoine [d.1960], in 1935, had been the first). While clearly influenced by Le Corbusier and Robert Mallet-Stevens (1886–1945), a major proponent of cubic forms in buildings, the building owes an even greater debt to the interior design of the great ocean liners of the era. Indeed the building has been described as a 'liner at anchor' (Michell and Martinelli, 1994; Raulet, 1996). (The Sen house in Calcutta, known locally as Jahaz Kothi, designed by Arjun Roy is more literally ship-like). The palace is an archetypal Moderne Art Deco building. Rectangular in its plan it encloses two courtyards surrounded by colonnades. Each courtyard has a central fountain. It is the interiors that remain stunning to this day with their free-flowing curvilinear forms and bright colours (Michell and Martinelli, 1994). Like the cinemas, the palace has retained its character in the present.

The Art Deco office buildings were much simpler than the cinemas and palaces and were visually closer to the modified classicism that was the norm for such buildings in the 1920s. The strong vertical ribs of the New India Assurance

The Sen House, Calcutta

The New India Assurance Building, Mumbai

Building (1935) designed by Master, Sathe and Bhuta, with N.G. Pansare as the artist, has a monumental quality, appearing larger than it is. Not only was the building modern in appearance, it was modern in its reinforced concrete structure. It also had an efficient layout and forced-air cooling. Horizontal projecting surfaces protect the building from the eastern and western sun, and, sensibly, central airshafts and operable windows allow for potential power failures. The electrical and plumbing work is in ducts. The Mercantile Bank of India Limited (1942) on Mahatma Gandhi Road in Mumbai (designed primarily by John Ritchie and L. Palfi) is, perhaps, more typical of the period. It contains classical as well as Art Deco elements. All these buildings were international in character. Efforts were also made to localise the Art Deco with referents to India. The result was an architecture which has come to be known as the Indo-Deco (Tillotson, 1989).

The Indo-Deco

During the 1930s an increased awareness of indigenous cultures led to the inclusion of local precedents in Art Deco forms. In the United States, for instance, mouldings and friezes started to include Pueblo and other elements perceived to be native-American. The integration of local elements and Art Deco motifs displayed in the Indo-Deco is more complex than in many other countries because of the diversity of India's architectural background. The elements borrowed from traditional house forms included sloping overhangs, corbelling and cement jaalis. Not only were Hindu and Islamic elements used but also elements of the country's colonial heritage. Patterns in Art Deco murals varied from abstract swastika patterns to representations of Indian legends and myths. Many of the murals owed a considerable debt to Aubrey Beardsley (1872–98), the British artist, in the eroticism of their lines and forms. Indian craftsmen picked up these patterns with enthusiasm.

The Mutual Insurance Building in Mumbai by Master, Sathe and Bhuta and the design for the Umaid Bhavan Palace in Jodhpur (1929–44) by Henry Vauhan Lanchaster (1863–1953) show a similar mixture of ideas. The Palace has strong Civic Baroque overtones, but does incorporate 'archaic architectural forms' and has the elegance of the Art Deco (Tillotson, 1989). A common feature of these examples is the integration of art and architecture.

The Kirti Mandir in Vadodara has murals by Nandalal Bose (1883–1966) that display the flowing lines of the Art Deco although the building itself owes more to the earlier Indo-Saracenic work in the city by Charles Mant (1840–80) and Robert Chisholm (1840–1915). The reliefs on the Mutual Insurance Building in Mumbai are closer to the Art Deco than the building itself. The Umaid Bhavan and Morvi Palaces have murals by Stephan Norbin de la Gordaine (1882–1952) in Art Deco form that display scenes from the *Ramayana* (McManus, 1993).

Perhaps the greatest burst of uniquely Indo-Deco architecture came not from someone based in India but from an American husband-wife team based in Australia. Walter Burley Griffin (1876–1937) and Marion Mahony Griffin (1871–1961) had been closely associated with Frank Lloyd Wright in Chicago at the beginning of the twentieth century, but had lived in Australia since Walter won the competition for the design of the country's new capital, Canberra. A Theosophist and thus sympathetic to India's political aspirations, Burley Griffin came to India in late 1935 after his design for the University of Lucknow Library had been accepted. Mahony followed in mid-May the year after. The Griffins' initial contact with India had been established through an Australian journalist working in India and later through a building contractor, Algappan Mudalar (Weirick, 1988; Tillotson, 1989; Kruty, 1998).

The Griffins clearly thought that the universalism of the International Modernism that was emerging in Europe was not appropriate for India on both climatic and cultural grounds. In contrast, the Griffins' work in the country showed a fusion of the massing and lines of the Art Deco and Indian decorative forms. Burley Griffin designed an office building for the *Pioneer* newspaper and an agricultural and industrial exposition to accompany the provincial election to be held under the Government of India Act of 1935. Other commissions followed these two: a library (1937) to house the Husainya collection of the Raja of Mahmudabad, a student union for the University of Lucknow (1937) and a number of private houses. The domestic work included the Raja Tagore House, the Sahni House, and the Narian Singh House in Varanasi all designed in 1936. For Ahmedabad, he designed a Town Hall (1936) at the instigation of Mudalar.

The Husainya Collection Library, never built, consisted of a series of superimposed masses with high windows set within receding planes. The theme was picked up in the terraces on which the building stands. The mud hut forms of the local villages inspired the design. As such, the thinking reflects the aristocratic-folklore ideas associated with the swaraj movement three decades earlier (Lang, Desai and Desai, 1997).

The design of the Town Hall building for Ahmedabad (one of the first designs that Griffin executed totally in India) clearly reflects his desire to have a public building that was both modern and Indian. The design was composed of balconies, verandahs, chabutras, screened walkways, receding and advancing planes, and unadorned and modified Mughal arches taken out into gable ends (Kruty, 1998). The design is strikingly different from that built to Claude Batley's design.

Indo-Deco architecture continued to be designed well into the 1960s. The Ramakrishna Mission (1957–62) in Calcutta designed by William B. Ker of Ballardie, Thompson and Matthews shows a blend of Art Deco, Modernist and traditional Indian elements as does the firm's design of the Akshvani Bhavan (All India Radio Building) in that city. On the whole, the firm's contemporary work showed an eclectic debt to Luytens, the Art Deco and Walter Gropius. Little of

The Ahmedabad Town Hall, proposal

The Akashvani Bhavan, Calcutta

it had the clarity of an architectural idea that their earlier Reid House still possesses.

What impact the Griffins' explorations would have had on Indian architecture if more of it had been built and if in 1937 Walter Burley Griffin had not died of peritonitis in Lucknow remains a conjecture. Only the zenana quarters for the Raja of Jahangirabad and one or two homes were completed. The work for the *Pioneer* was demolished in 1991 and what was built for the exposition hardly reflects the Griffins' ideas; neither do the zenana quarters. The Griffins are now all but forgotten in India and the contemporary work of a small number of other foreign architects in what is generally known as the Modernist idiom, has survived little better in architects' minds.

INTERNATIONAL MODERNISM

International Modernism, born of the Rationalist spirit of continental Europe, was the core of avant-garde international architectural practice from 1920 to 1960. It has remained the basis for much subsequent work. One of the first International Modernist buildings was the Fagus shoelace factory at Alfeld-an-der-Leine (1911) by Walter Gropius (1883–1969) and Adolf Meyer (1881–1929). It is three-storeyed, steel framed and has glass-screen walls. The non-structural nature of the walls is emphasised by the lack of vertical supports at the corners. As head of the Staatliche Bauhaus, Gropius was designer of a number of buildings including the best known of his works, the Bauhaus complex (1925–6) at Dessau. While his buildings are important, his reshaping of art and industrial design education has probably been his major contribution to the design world (Fitch, 1960; Wingler, 1969).

Gropius assembled a team of educators that, for good or ill, redesigned the way architectural education has since been conducted. With the coming of Nazism, many members of the group left Germany. László Moholy-Nagy (1895–1946) went to the New Bauhaus in Chicago, Josef Albers (1888–1976), to Yale, Gropius himself to Harvard via London (where he worked with Maxwell Fry) and Ludwig Mies van de Rohe (1886–1969) went to Chicago. Their impact on American architectural education and practice and later on Indian architecture was substantial. The Bauhaus was not, however, the only influential source of Modernist architectural ideas.

Le Corbusier's thinking of the period was similar to the Bauhaus ideology. His proposed city for three million inhabitants (1922), his design for the Maison Suisse in the Cité Universitaire, Paris (1930–2) and the Citrohan Houses proposals (1920–2) all show the reduction of buildings to the basic geometric shapes of rectilinear, plane surfaces, cubes and, sometimes, cylinders. The buildings often stand on pilotes and have strips of fenestration, glass walls and flat roofs. When designed as complexes, Le Corbusier proposed that buildings be set apart from each other, turn their sides to streets and be surrounded by open space as objects in a field (Le Corbusier, 1963).

Walter Burley Griffin noted 'a hankering' for a stark Modernist architecture amongst Indian architects, but there is only sparse evidence that they were willing to follow this line of thought and more that they were opposed to it (Deshpande, 1939; Kshirasagar, 1941; Batley, 1954). While a number of architects in India did begin to explore Modernist architectural ideas during the 1930s and 1940s, it can hardly be claimed that there was any concerted effort to produce International Style buildings in the country.

The Fagus Shoe Factory, Alfeld-an-der-Leine, Germany

Maison Suisse, Paris

Some work for the Calico Mills in Ahmedabad by Asarpota and Asarpota shows the influence of contemporary ideas of the purist school of European Rationalism. The Shodhan House (1939; now demolished) by Atmaram Gajjar (1901–61) in that city had a plan that showed the evolving ways of life of the

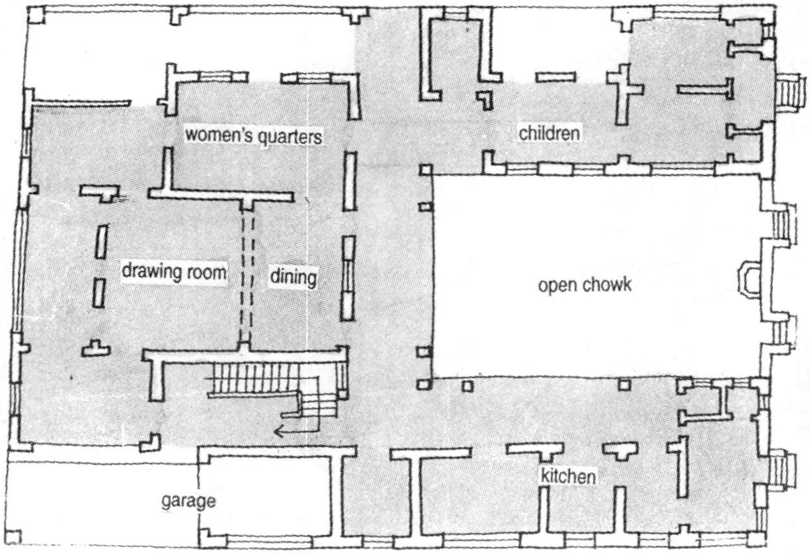

The Shodhan House, Ahmedabad, plan

The Shodhan House, Ahmedabad

Indian upper-classes and façades that presented a simple Modernist face to the world. In the suburbs of Mumbai there are a number of houses by graduates of the Sir J.J. School that were inspired by the work of Frank Lloyd Wright. G.B. Mhatre's design for Sunayan (1943) is a departure from his Art Deco work and shows that Indian architects were familiar with Frank Lloyd Wright's organic designs. Today, Sunayan appears to be a side step in the transition of Mhatre's work from the Art Deco to the International Modernist flavour of the Marble Arch Apartments (1950–5).

Despite these examples, the truly Modernist buildings erected in India during the 1930s and early 1940s were the isolated work of foreign architects unconnected with Indian architectural firms. These architects worked for wealthy clients with strong international outlooks on life. They included Eckhart Muthesius, Willem Marinus Dudok (1884–1974), Antonin Raymond (1888–1976) and Otto Koenigsberger (1909–99). Chronologically, Frank Lloyd Wright could be included in the list because his proposal for the Calico Mills office building was executed in 1946. The building is, however, part of another story so will be considered later. Of these architects only Koenigsberger had a significant personal association with India, spending over a decade in the country, and becoming an Indian citizen (something he cherished throughout his life) before moving on to London. Dudok seems never to have visited India.

Muthesius designed the new Indore Palace, a railway carriage and a houseboat (as a floating palace), for Maharaja Manik Bagh during the 1930s (Pica, 1979). The palace, in particular, is imbued with Rationalist ideas. The symmetrical building has a U-shaped plan around an open courtyard. The interior used to be similarly simple and was complemented by the functionalist furniture of Charlotte Perriand (b.1903), a member of Le Corbusier's atelier in Paris from 1927 to 1935. The building has been much changed over the years and the furniture auctioned off (Raulet, 1996).

Dudok designed just one major building in India, Calcutta's Garden Theatre and Lighthouse Cinema (1936–8), and, possibly, one house. The theatre/cinema, now much altered, still recalls the De Stijl work of Dutch architects of the period. The building's bold contrasts between solid surfaces and voids, between vertical and horizontal lines and its use of balconies and circular windows (now largely gone) are clearly within the De Stijl mould. Known to local architects, the building seems to have had very little influence on the Calcutta architectural scene although there are glimpses of similar thinking in buildings such as the Lady Dufferin Memorial Hospital (1937), a work of Ballardie, Thompson and Matthews (Tafel, 1945). European De Stijl influences can also be seen in houses of the 1940s and 1950s in areas such as Golf Links and Sundar Nagar in New Delhi but such influence can be attributed to neither Dudok nor the Lighthouse Cinema (Dalal, 2000). Dudok's building was largely unknown outside Calcutta. Golconde is much better known.

Indore Palace

Galconde (1936–48; French for Golconda, the citadel located outside Hyderabad) was designed by Raymond for the ashram of Aurobindo Ghosh (1872–1950) in Pondicherry. Raymond came to India from Japan where he had worked for Frank Lloyd Wright and where he was one of the earliest Modernists. Despite his experiences with Frank Lloyd Wright his own work is strictly International Modernist in both spirit and execution. The reinforced concrete building has a strikingly simple form. Its use of cross ventilation, pre-cast horizontal louvres and precast thin-shell vaulting that forms a double roof for insulation deals well with the climate. More importantly, it demonstrates a new concept of spatial organisation and so may well be considered to be the first Modernist building in India (Dormitory, 1951; M. Chatterjee, 1985). The American architect George Nakashima

The Lighthouse, Calcutta

(1905–90), later to receive international recognition for his woodcraftsmanship, was Raymond's collaborator on the project, arriving in Pondicherry before Raymond and leaving after him (Raymond, 1973).

The Dining Hall, the Indian Institute of Sciences, Bangalore

Galconde, Pondicherry

Koenigsberger, a Schinkle prize winner in Germany, came to India in 1939, a refugee from Hitler's tyranny. Koenigsberger was Government Architect in Mysore until 1948 and thereafter, until 1952, he was housing adviser to the Government of India. His design for the Dining Hall of the Indian Institute of Science in Bangalore (1947) possesses the simplicity of line and form that is characteristic of the work of Bruno Taut (1869–1936) and Hans Poelzig (1880–1938) while his design for Bangalore's Sri Jaya Chamarajendra Victory Hall (1946) owes more to German Expressionism. It is as a town planner rather than as an architect that Koenigsberger left his mark on India. He was responsible for the plan (but not the architecture) of Bhubaneswar in Orissa and the master plans for cities such as Jamshedpur in Bihar (Koenigsberger, 1952).

The work of Muthesius, Dudok, Raymond, and even Koenigsberger, had little immediate impact on subsequent architecture in India. Its effect was probably subtle and indirect. For instance, Raymond's and Nakashima's enthusiasm for India was instrumental to Bernard Kohn (b.1929) coming to India in the 1960s. Koenigsberger is now remembered in the country for his later research on tropical architecture. By the time his architectural work had escaped the demands of his clients 'for domes', the work of the first generation of Indian modernists was beginning to make an impact on the Indian scene and the revivalist ideas of the Modern Indian Architectural Movement were already beginning to be forgotten.

A REACTION: THE MODERN INDIAN ARCHITECTURAL MOVEMENT

The Modern Indian Architectural Movement represented a bold and radical departure from the mainstream of contemporary architectural thinking both in India and the world. Revivalist in presentation but often progressive in spirit, the architecture represents the belief that the past can give order to the present and be a source of identity and pride for the people who see it as part of *their* culture. The search for an Indianness or even an Indian regional architecture was explicit in a number of works during the 1920s and 1930s. The early buildings at Benares Hindu University, a hotbed of Indian nationalism, exemplify this search. The Osmania University buildings of the 1930s in Hyderabad are others that represent the quest.

The College of Arts building (1934) at Osmania University is a blend of Arab, Moorish and even Gothic elements and was overtly designed to stand apart symbolically and overtly from the British-founded tertiary educational institutions in India (Raza, 1953). While its design had roots in the proposals of a Belgian architect, the Hyderabad State architect Nawab Zain Yar Jung ultimately executed it. Although similar historical influences were the basis of the Modern Indian Architecture Movement, the symbolic aesthetic referents that the Movement advocated were different. Hyderabad being a predominantly Muslim state, the symbolic elements were drawn from the Islamic architectural heritage. Similar in architectural attitude, the Modern Indian Architectural Movement was, however, clearly Hindu.

Sris Chandra Chatterjee (1873–1966) was the moving force behind the Movement. Its ideology was an explicit reaction to Art Deco in India, to the developments of International Modernism on the European scene, and to what was seen to be happening in Japan where Western influences had had a significant impact on architecture. While the proposals of the movement had strong antecedents in the Indo-Saracenic work of people such as Colonel Sir Swinton Jacob (1841–1917), its purposes differed. While the Indo-Saracenic was an effort by British architects to display a concern for India through design, Chatterjee was motivated by the politics of the swadeshi movement of the first two decades of the twentieth century (Gupta, 1991; Oza, 1995).

During the 1930s, Chatterjee, a staunch supporter of the Congress Party, was a member of the National Planning Committee headed by Jawaharlal Nehru. Earlier, he had worked for the Public Works Departments of Bengal and Bikaner. The Lallgarh Palace (1895–1902) for Maharaja Ganga Singh in Bikaner was one of Jacob's major works and Chatterjee must have been familiar with it. He was certainly an admirer of Bombay's General Post Office (1902) designed by John Begg (1866–1937) (Gupta, 1991).

In urban design, Chatterjee turned to the canonical texts, particularly the *Shilpa Shastras* to establish the bases for his designs. For his architectural inspiration he turned to the glories of 'Magadha, Ajanta and Ellora, Mamallapuram and Conjeevaram, Dilwara and Vijayanagar' (S.C. Chatterjee, 1942). His work seems to be more a pastiche—a patching together of components—than a synthesis of the design principles that informed the historical work, although in urban design he stuck close to the canonical texts. His generic design for an Indian Village for 5,000 people consists of a rectangular plan with formal entrance gates on each side—a *chaturmukha* design. (Interestingly, in June 2000, the Gujarat government sanctioned money for building appropriate gates to all the villages in the state.) Chatterjee's design is predominantly a housing proposal with a central temple, community hall, social training centre and other public facilities. While his urban designs may have been based on Indian canonical principles, they also appear to be very much in the contemporary English garden city tradition with Beaux Arts overtones. Spatially, they are certainly appropriate for hot humid climates (Oza, 1995).

In architecture, Chatterjee executed a small body of work that clearly illustrated his goals. During the 1930s, he designed the Lakshmi-Narayan (Birla) Temple (1938) and the Mahasabha Bhavan (1939) both in Delhi, the Arya Dharma Sangha Dharamsala (1935) in Sarnath and the Deshbandhu Memorial to the Bengali patriot and politician Chittaranjan Das (1870–1925) in Calcutta. His design of 'a house for an Indian nobleman' shows where his architectural heart lay, while the Ashok Singh Palace (c.1942) in Calcutta is an example of his

The Arts College, Osmania University, Hyderabad

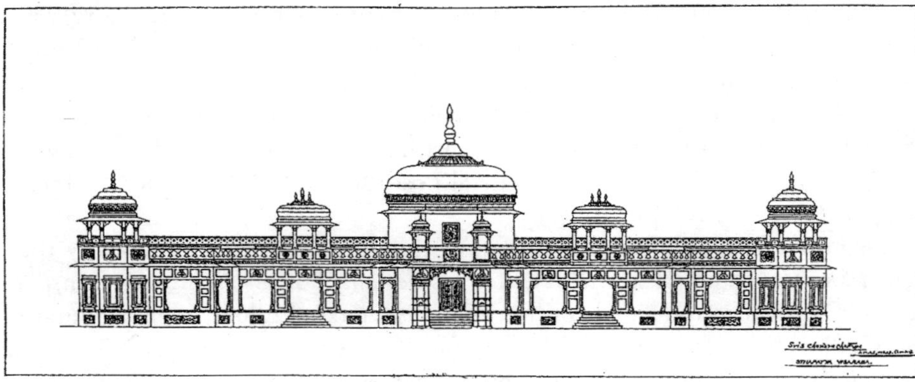

A house for an Indian nobleman

Ashok Singh Palace, Calcutta

executed domestic architecture. All are revivalist. The temple has antecedents in the temples of Bhubaneswar (although its administrative and social organisation was totally modern) and the dharamsala borrows elements of Buddhist architecture to cater to the pilgrims coming to Sarnath. Despite the appearance of the buildings, he was quite willing to use modern construction materials such as concrete. In 1940, Chatterjee published a manifesto for an 'All India League of Architects' to promote a new architecture for India based on historical principles (see Lang, Desai and Desai, 1997).

There were a number of reactions to Chatterjee's ideas. They received tacit, often guarded, support from a number of prominent people, Nehru amongst them (see S. C. Chatterjee, 1942). During the 1950s, Nehru, however, threw his support behind a very different architecture—that of Le Corbusier. The Modernists amongst Indian architects were vehemently opposed to Chatterjee's ideas and he was dismissed as 'a revivalist of the most retrogressive kind' (MARG, 1947). Chatterjee is important because his thinking is still with us and the desire to be Indian, *per se*, has almost always, but not inevitably, led to an architecture of at least a partial revivalism.

A REFLECTION

The Indian architectural profession as we know it today found its feet in the 1920s. The Indian Institute of Architects is modelled on its counterparts in Europe and North America. It could have evolved out of the mistri tradition but it did not. It is idle now to speculate on what form the role of designers would have taken if it had evolved out of the latter. What we have is a modern institution for a modern country.

It must be remembered that professional architects were responsible for the design of only a tiny fraction of buildings in India. Most buildings were designed by mistris. The mistris were, however, influenced by what architects were doing and were adopting new modes of construction and management. At the same time, the amount of Art Deco work in India showed that times were changing. The isolated examples of Modernist work and the letters in the *Journal of the Indian Institute of Architects* suggest that India was on the path not only to a new political future but also to new lines of architectural thought. Nevertheless, the twins tugs of looking back to the past and looking forward to a rationally designed future had established themselves as the forces that would long pull at the hearts and minds of Indian architects.

If in Europe it was the end of World War Two that signalled a new optimism about the future and a desire to create a new world, in India it was political independence. First, for a brief period, the country was a British dominion with Nehru as Prime Minister and Lord Mountbatten (1900–79), the last Viceroy, as Governor-General and then it chose to be an independent republic politically unallied to any world power. In architecture, however, the ideas were closely allied to those of the West.

The New Secretariat, Calcutta

3

The First Generation of Modernist Architecture: 1945 to 1970

THE FIRST two decades of Independence saw nothing close to the technological and social change of the prior two decades. What did occur was three fold: 1) the widespread dissemination of those earlier changes; 2) the founding of many new institutions as a result of political independence, and 3) mammoth new housing programs. The last was partly because of the influx of Hindus into India after Partition and partly a result of the natural increase in population. It was in this context that Modernist architecture took off in India.

Three sets of architects and architecture concern us here. First, there was the work of the firms whose architecture evolved from a somewhat conservative 1930s outlook towards a Modernist approach. Second, and intellectually allied to those firms, were the Indian architects whose work had grown out of the Art Deco. Third, and more influentially, there was the work of the Indian architects who received their education abroad during the post-Second World War burst of enlightenment thinking. This third group is the most interesting here because its members set the intellectual pace for Indian architecture during the first three decades of Independence. It is the work of the first two groups, however, that set the scene.

THE ARCHITECTURAL BACKGROUND

The defeat of Nazism and Fascism saw a Europe looking for a new direction. In India, the securing of political independence in 1947 was accompanied by a similar search. One available alternative was the Gandhian philosophy of a simple life and the restoration of village India as the foundation of the future country, and the other, Nehru's image of a socialist, industrialised modern India, free of poverty and unfettered by past constraints. Gandhi's dream was impossible to realise: too much had changed. Nehru's dream has also been illusory.

With Independence and the gradual departure of British engineers and architects, Indian professionals took over the major firms and the leadership roles in the Public Works Departments [PWDs], a process that had begun in the 1930s. In the short term, it resulted in little change in the nature of the architecture because most of the new leaders had been trained under British tutelage. Although he died in Mumbai in 1956, it was the architectural ghost of Claude Batley that influenced much Indian architecture during the era.

Most major Indian architects of the period were either educated under Claude Batley at the Sir J.J. School of Architecture in Mumbai or worked with him in Gregson, Batley and King [GBK]. The Sir J.J. School produced some of the finest architects in India and GBK was, essentially, the Indian post-graduate design school from the 1920s well into the 1950s and even beyond. A great concern of both the school and the firm was to produce architecture that was modern, with symbolic referents to India, and suitable for the existing ways of life as well as the climate of the country. There is greater sympathy for these goals today than there was amongst many of the young Modernists of the 1950s.

It was not simply the established private firms who were responsible for the emerging professionally designed built environment. The Public Works Departments [PWDs] played an even greater role in shaping the physical environment of early post-Independence India. Most of the PWDs' architectural work of the period was an amalgam of the work they had produced during the 1930s and the images of modern buildings, particularly housing, seeping into architectural journals. It was not until Habib Rahman (1916–96) joined the Central PWD [CPWD] that a new direction was discernible and for a long time he was a lone wolf amongst CPWD architects. The work of the Orissa PWD in Bhubaneswar, the CPWD, and that of the erstwhile Mysore state in the design of Vidhana Soudha can serve as exemplars of the various directions the Public Works Departments took.

The Early Modernist Work of the Established Architectural Firms

During the 1940s and 1950s the major firms, both British- and Indian-headed, that had established themselves in the 1930s and 1940s developed a commercial modification of the Internationalist Modernist genre of the 1930s. The adaptation occurred in two ways: first through the simplification of the Art Deco exuberance to meet Modernist demands and second, through the adaptation of the norms of International Modernism to the climatic natures and construction processes of India. The work of Ballardie, Thompson and Matthews in Calcutta exemplifies the former approach and the work of Walter George in New Delhi, the latter. What seems to have evolved out of a synthesis of the two approaches is the Utilitarian Modernism that characterises so much of the architectural work in India to this day.

The India Exchange Building (1950–1), the ICI (India) Office Building (1953) and the much earlier Lady Dufferin Victoria Hospital (1937), all in Calcutta, by Ballardie, Thompson and Matthews, show the influence of International Modernism on the Art Deco. The designers of record for much of the firm's work were William Leseaz and William Kerr. The main block of the Indian Institute of Technology in Kharagpur (1951) designed by the practice is a simple modern building typical of the work of the British-headed companies and their descendants. The building is still favoured as a work location, on comfort grounds if none else, in comparison with the 1970s and 1980s Modernist buildings that surround it on the campus. George's design for the Tuberculosis Association Building (1950–2), with its use of lightweight horizontal louvres, his Lodi Colony housing of the late 1940s and his design for Sujan Singh Park show a strikingly Modernist

The Carmichael Apartments, Mumbai

touch. The same touch can be seen in the contemporary work of a number of other firms as in the Glaxo Laboratories offices and godown in Mumbai designed by W.W. Wood and Sons and Partners.

The Indian-headed firms were also following similar lines of tentative Modernist design in their work. The Carmichael Apartments (1937) by Kushro P. Burjo-Behram and Hermasji J. Billimoria may show a love of the Art Deco but it is clearly a more Modernist building in outlook. The Siliguri Railway Station (1948–50) designed by Nariman Bejonji Shroff, another graduate of GBK, reflects both the work of Batley and the purist generation of Modernists. Similar ambiguities pervade the architecture of the Public Works Departments, at both Central and State level.

The Central PWD and the Designing of New Delhi

Ganesh Bhikaji Deolalikar (1890–1979) was the first Indian to head the Central Public Works Department in New Delhi [CPWD]. Shridhar Krishna Joglekar, a graduate of GBK, was the next. They faced the problems of how to develop the Mall area of New Delhi in response to the needs of an expanding democratic government which required new administrative and institutional buildings. They faced a quandary given the strong urban design and architectural precedents set by Lutyens and Baker. The Modernists took the position that the precedents were largely irrelevant and, on political if not aesthetic grounds, should not be heeded in the development of the city. The attitude is displayed, for instance, in the siting of the Carpenter Centre (1960) designed by Le Corbusier for Harvard University. An antagonism to the existing order, social, urban and architectural, was regarded as a prerequisite for creative design. The CPWD, however, decided to build to the existing order.

The goal in developing the Mall was to fit in with the architecture of Luytens and Baker without being the same. Many of the buildings that align or are adjacent to the Mall today, such as the Supreme Court (1952), Vigyan Bhavan (1962), Krishi Bhavan (c.1957), Udyog Bhavan (1957) and Rail Bhavan (1962) use chhajjas and chhattris and are topped by domes. Today they are seen to be, and indeed really are, heavy-handed attempts to capture the essence of Lutyens' work. The resources in terms of skills and finances available to the early post-Independence CPWD architects were considerably more limited than those available to their British ancestors.

Deolalikar designed the Supreme Court in an Indo-British style. It is topped by a dome following the precedent set by Lutyens in the design of the Viceroy's Palace. It has chhattris on 15-inch [380-mm] square supports that stand in strong contrast to those in the designs by Lutyens or Baker and those, for instance, at Fatehpur Sikri. Brick and stucco are no substitute for stone. Other elements of

The Supreme Court, New Delhi

The Vigyan Bhavan, New Delhi

the Indian architectural heritage combined with the simplicity of Modernist forms were used as the basis for design in many PWD buildings.

The Vigyan Bhavan (1955) designed by R.I. Gehlote of the CPWD was built for international conferences. Its façades contain elements of Hindu and Mughal architecture but its massing and simplicity of form following Modernist principles give the building an overall modern air despite its revivalist components. The large entrance of black marble and glass borrows its form from the chaitya arches of Ajanta although its scale and springing lines differ. The windows, being similar, give a unity to the whole composition. The building is topped by a perforated jaali; a chhajja below runs the length of the building's façade.

As often favoured in the designs for major buildings by the British architects before them, Buddhist design elements are prominent in Sapru House, designed by the CPWD for the Indian Council of World Affairs. The building has a dome in the form of the stupa at Sanchi below which is the main stair and *porte cochere*. The side wings are, however, a subdued Modernist 'form follows function' endeavour. The juxtaposition of Indian antecedents with the clean lines of Modernist architecture is even clearer in the Azad Bhavan (1958–61) designed for the Indian Centre for Cultural Relationships by Achyut Kanvinde (b.1916). Important though such institutional buildings are, the bulk of Public Works Department work in New Delhi as in other cities, was housing, particularly mass housing.

If in their design of major buildings in New Delhi the architects of the CPWD were influenced by Lutyens and Baker, in their more mundane work they showed a familiarity with European Rationalist ideas (Dalal, 2000). Housing in such areas as Kaka Nagar, Bapa Nagar, Sarojini Nagar and Laxmibai Nagar show a remarkable similarity to that illustrated in *Une Cité Industrielle* (1901–4; published 1917) by Tony Garnier (1869–1948), a key French Modernist on whose ideas both Le Corbusier and the Bauhaus drew.

Vast housing areas were built by the CPWD and later the Delhi Development Authority [DDA]. In addition to Kaka Nagar, Bapa Nagar, and Sarojini Nagar, amongst the other products of the era are Nizamuddin, Lajpat Nagar, Kalkaji and Malaviya Nagar, two Rajendra Nagars, three Patel Nagars, Moti Nagar, Ramesh Nagar and Tilak Nagar.

Laxmibai Nagar is typical of middle income housing projects built by the CPWD in the 1950s. It was erected for government employees. It consists of 756 three-room flats for gazetted workers and 665 two-bedroom units for the non-gazetted. Following basic neighbourhood unit design principles, a school is located at the centre of the development and a market in a corner. The blocks of housing are organised around open areas that serve as parks and for the parking of cars. The architecture is simple, with the stair towers of the two-storey structures being accentuated vertically. Thin, flat concrete slabs project over porches, windows and external door openings to provide shelter from the sun. The complex was not designed to be an architectural statement as, say, was the Weissenhof housing

Housing, Une Cité Industrielle

Housing, Bapa Nagar, New Delhi

Laxmibai Nagar, New Delhi

scheme (1926–7) by Walter Gropius (Fitch, 1960). The goal of the CPWD was modest—to provide salubrious, reasonably comfortable shelter in symbolically acceptable settings. They sought no architectural accolades.

After 1960, the housing began to be built at higher density levels. It became more uniform and followed more closely Modernist siting principles, being in rows rather than enclaves. The buildings were usually four storeys high and stuccoed. Jaalis and other motifs were used to give them a local touch. The appearance of the mass housing designed during this period was similar from one end of India to the other. The similarity can be seen, for instance, in the design of the housing in Bhubaneswar, the first of the new capital cities of independent India. The design of the capital complex there, however, shows the dilemma facing Indian architects after Independence. What architectural path should we follow?

The Orissa PWD and the Design of Bhubaneswar

The state of Orissa was formed from parts of the presidencies of Bengal and Madras in 1933, with Cuttack as its capital. A new capital site was already being sought before the British quit India. After Independence, open land near the ancient temple city of Bhubaneswar was selected for the new town. The scheme was pushed ahead by Hare Krishna Mahatab (1899–1965), the Chief Minister of Orissa, who wanted the state's capital to be a new temple city spatially and architecturally. He did not get it.

The planner for the site was Otto Koenigsberger and the architect Julius Vaz. Koenigsberger designed the plan along the Empiricist lines of British and American garden city models with separate neighbourhood units acting as residential and service areas for local populations. Each unit was to provide the essential amenities for life: schools, shopping centres, clinics, and libraries, all within the walking distance of a young schoolchild. A central artery acted as a spine for the city (Koenigsberger, 1952; Kalia, 1994) so that further growth could take place in a linear fashion. There was also a social engineering agenda. Neither caste nor economic segregation were to exist; gender equality and education were to be stressed.

The architectural character of Bhubaneswar exhibits a particular line of thought prevalent during the late 1940s about what modern architecture for India should be (Vaz, 1954). The Secretariat (*c.*1950+) is an interesting combination of Art Deco and International Modernist architecture with Revivalist touches. Its central tower is similar in aspiration to the cinemas of Mumbai while the wings of the building are Utilitarian Modernist. The projecting thin concrete fins emphasise the vertical nature of the tower while the more mundane pattern of windows in the wings divided by less bold fins butting into a thin cornice are more narrowly functional. They allow almost any configuration of offices behind them.

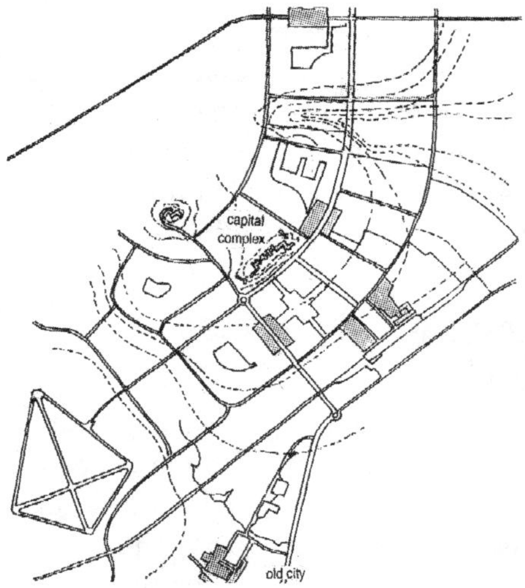

Bhubaneswar, plan

The Secretariat, Bhubaneswar

The Market Place, Bhubaneswar

The Orissa State Museum (1954), a later design by Vaz, also reveals a Modernist touch illustrating the versatility of many Indian architects in adapting design approaches to their clients' specifications. Both buildings are reinforced concrete column and slab structures with infill panels. Neither has evidence of the spatial explorations that were to come to India once the influence of Le Corbusier's work in the country became widespread. Vaz's design for the market is more Revivalist in nature, incorporating many traditional Buddhist elements.

Koenigsberger had wanted Bhubaneswar to be a Modernist city, but by the time its development began he was ensconced in New Delhi. If he had had his way, Bhubaneswar might have been a city to architecturally rival Chandigarh. If Mahatab had got his way, the capital complex might have rivalled the Vidhana Soudah in Bangalore. Either way, a bolder result would have ensued. Would it have been more livable too?

The Mysore State PWD and the Vidhana Soudha

In the state of Mysore, Kengal Hanumanthiah (1908–80), a staunch regionalist who was Chief Minister from 1950 to 1956, took great interest in the design of the Vidhana Soudha (1952–7). The Vidhana Soudha is now the legislative and administrative centre of the state of Karnataka. Seen by its designers as a modern building for modern India, it is *the* exemplar of a revivalist building of the era. The chief architect of the building was B.R. Manickam, a civil engineer and town planner, with Hanumanthia Rao Naidu, a graduate of London's Architectural Association, as his assistant. It is, however, clearly Kengal Hanumanthiah's building. He wanted not only an Indian building but one characteristic of the region, and he got it! Today, his statue, building model in hand, stands proudly before the members' entrance to the building.

While the massing, proportional systems and the general layout of the Vidhan Soudha, with its grand central steps leading to a portico and the dome above are

The Vidhana Soudha, Bangalore

European Classical in character, the detailing is neo-Dravidian. The four-storey plus basement building is massive in plan (220 by 150 metres) and bulk. The central dome rises to 55 metres above ground level and there are subsidiary domes. Surrounding verandahs cater for the climate. It is constructed of structural granite except for the central dome which stands on reinforced concrete columns.

The decorative elements of the building—chhajjas, column capitals and brackets—are drawn from temple architecture. Yet the building is no mere copy of the past but a carefully orchestrated design. Masons capable of working the stone in a traditional Dravidian manner had to be recruited from as far afield as Karaikul and Tiruchirapalli. They completed a building which would be almost impossible to replicate nowadays. Neither the finances nor the workmen would be easy to find.

A number of works of the 1990s and early 2000 are being built in the same revivalist tradition. They are considerably less grand in overall massing and in elaboration. Amongst them are the Sri Sathya Sai Institute of Higher Medicinal Science in Puttaparthi (1992+) designed by local architects in conjunction with Keith Critchlow, a British architect; and the M.S. Ramaiah Institute in Bangalore (1990+) designed largely, it appears, by contractor-builders. Few revivalist buildings are as rich in nature as the Vidhana Soudha.

The Impact of the Leading Architectural Firms and the PWDs

The work of the 1930s and 1940s and the contemporary work of the leading firms and PWDs during the 1950s exerted considerable influence on other architects. Even the influence of Lutyens persisted. It can be seen, for example, in the main complex of Gujarat University (1947) designed by Atmaram Gajjar. The symmetrical stone building has a domed clock-tower typical of the British contribution to India. The design for the Senate House (1956) of Kerala University in Thiruvananthapuram (Trivandrum) by S.L. Chitale (b.1932) has a similar mixture of the old and the new.

In many of the buildings of the era, traditional elements were used to locate a predominantly Modernist building in its context. The Ashok Hotel (1955) in New Delhi is really a modern building that is adorned with traditional elements. It was designed by E.B. Doctor (1900–84), a Mumbai based architect and a professor at the Sir J.J. School. While it is like any other contemporary international five-star hotel inside, its façade has jaali work and huge jharokhas that are cantilevered out and supported by brackets. Against the skyline are a series of chhattris.

Modernists regarded such eclecticism as intellectually dishonest because of the lack of unity in its internal logic. Nevertheless, such design efforts have become more generally acceptable as the limitations of Modernist ideology have emerged. Rajasthan, for example, is being increasingly 'Rajasthanified' by the use of

The Senate House, Kerala University, Thiruvananthapuram

The Ashok Hotel, New Delhi

traditional elements in many new buildings, public and private. While such efforts are probably unnecessary in establishing a sense of place, lay people—locals and tourists alike—readily understand them. In the 1950s and 1960s, however, it was the boldness of architectural form and the internal logic of Rationalist design arguments that captured the hearts and minds of a new generation of Indian architects.

THE FIRST MODERNIST GENERATION

The years after the Second World War were the years in which socialist political values gained preeminence in Europe and, with the achieving of their independence, in former colonial countries across the world. In India, it was the era of Nehru and it was his vision for the newly independent country, rather than Gandhi's, that not only motivated Indians but also inspired much of the world. The Rationalist philosophy that was Nehru's also filled the hearts of young architects. They were dreaming about future possibilities.

It was primarily to the United States that young Indian, particularly northern Indian, architects looked for inspiration and for their postgraduate education. America was seen as *the* modern country and with political independence the easy dismissal of American attitudes that was characteristic of many British intellectual circles began to be unimportant to Indians. The United States was seen as the intellectual as well as political powerhouse of the English-speaking world.

First generation Modernist architecture in India was also the product of a number of a highly influential young foreign architects who came to India to bolster architectural education at a time when it was searching for a new direction. On the one hand there was new architecture to observe; on the other, such work was often prescribed as the model in architectural schools. The dual impact set in place the changes that affected the nature of buildings in India for the next thirty years—until the 1980s, when the challenge to the Modernist paradigm could no longer be ignored.

The Indian Architects

The paucity of Indian architects and the vast amount of construction required in the newly independent country meant that many young Indian architects were required to take up the challenge of working on projects way beyond the level that their experience would normally have warranted. Of these young architects, the first to have a lasting influence was Habib Rahman (1916–96). A Bengali engineer, he was the first of a number of Indians to study overseas under the supervision of internationally renowned Modernist architects. He attended the Massachusetts Institute of Technology [MIT] at both an undergraduate and postgraduate level completing his master's degree in 1944.

Achyut Kanvinde followed in Rahman's footsteps to Cambridge, Massachusetts, but to Harvard not MIT, finishing his studies in 1947. Cyrus S.H. Jhabvala (b.1920) studied in London, Vanu Bhuta (b.1922) attended the Institute of

Design in Chicago and studied with Eliel Saarinen at Cranbrook, Bennett Pithavadian (1922–98) attended McGill until 1951 studying with John Bland. Gautam Sarabhai (1917–95) and his sister, Gira Sarabhai (b.1923), worked at Taliesen with Frank Lloyd Wright during the 1940s. Mansinh M. Rana (b.1922) and Nari Gandhi (1934–93) followed them. Many other architects went to America during the 1950s. They included Pravina Mehta (*c.*1925–88) who attended the Illinois Institute of Technology, Charles Correa (b.1930) who went to Michigan and MIT, and Hasmukh Chandubhai Patel (b.1933) who attended Cornell. Ram Sharma (b.1934) went to Harvard and Pratt, and Piloo Mody studied with Erich Mendelsohn (1887–1953) at the University of Southern California. They led the way to a new architecture in India and, later, for India.

Diverse though the group was, it was unified in a number of ways. Its members worked for major architects while abroad; they travelled widely and were much influenced by Bauhaus thinking either directly by studying or working with Walter Gropius or his former colleagues, or indirectly by their writings. Rahman, for instance, worked for Lawrence Anderson, Ely Khan, Walter Gropius and Konrad Waschman. Charles Correa worked for Minoru Yamasaki (b.1912) in Detroit and Durga Bajpai for the great Finnish architect, Alvar Alto (1898–1976) in Helsinki. They had read books on architecture and were particularly enthused by the way Brazil had embraced Modernist thought. Kidder Smith's books (e.g., Smith, 1950) on the architecture of various countries seems to have featured prominently in their reading. They were unified by a desire to bring new approaches to architecture to a new India. Nevertheless, they remained an eclectic group and while their work clearly had the stamp of their respective mentors at the outset, it evolved considerably with their own experience in completing work and seeing it in place. One of the problems, to this day, is how to educate young aspiring architects to be problem-solvers rather than imitators of singular approaches, usually stylistic, picked up during their educations.

The International Architects

Walter George in New Delhi and Claude Batley in Mumbai were amongst the British architects who continued until their deaths to make major contributions to the design profession in India after Independence. Otto Koenigsberger stayed on until 1952. Other international architects designed a number of major buildings during the immediate post-Independence days. An Australian, John A. Ritchie, practising in Mumbai, designed the Reserve Bank of India in Calcutta. Holabird and Root of Chicago designed the Tata Centre in Calcutta. Willgoose and Chase of Washington DC designed the US Consulate Staff Quarters also in Calcutta. Most widely published has been the United States Embassy in New Delhi (1958) designed by Edward Durrell Stone (1902–78). It is one of a number of notable embassies built over the years in the Chanakyapuri district of New Delhi.

The United States Embassy, New Delhi

The Embassy is a modern classical building. The whole white rectangular composition with its slender gilded columns has a classical air but does not use classical features. It also has elements that relate it to its Indian context—an internal courtyard, elevated platforms and pierced walls—but their purposes are different. While the traditional use of these features in India was to deal with the climate, Stone's use was largely aesthetic. They function well in this manner and the building was very well received by the contemporary Indian press (Evenson, 1989).

Most of these international architects came and went, but a few have made a more permanent contribution to India. The most prominent among them was Joseph Allen Stein (1912–2001) both as an early educator and, more prominently, as a practitioner. He came to India to head the Department of Architecture at the Bengal School of Engineering in 1952 but within three years had established a practice in New Delhi with another American, Benjamin Polk (b.1916). Polk (with B.K. Chatterjee) had a flourishing practice in Calcutta and his work included the design of the new Senate House for Calcutta University. Later Stein had practices with other architects including Balkrishna V. Doshi (b.1927).

In the 1960s, Bernard Kohn, an American educated Frenchman, joined Doshi in co-directing the Centre for Environmental Planning and Technology [CEPT] in Ahmedabad. With the input of American architect Harry Weese (b.1915) they developed the educational program of one of the most-influential architectural academies anywhere. Christopher Benninger (b.1942), an American, came to India in 1968 and was the first Head of the School of Planning at CEPT in 1972. As an architect, he designed the Alliance Française Library (1973) while in Ahmedabad. He later continued his role as an educator at the Centre for Development Studies and Activities in Pune where he has an award-winning architectural practice. Kohn too designed a number of buildings in India: houses as well as the Satellite Tracking Building of the Space Applications Centre (1967–78; with Kanvinde, Rai and Chowdhuri) in Ahmedabad.

These architects were unified by an enthusiasm for India. They were drawn largely from the British and American experience rather than the European. In their work they drew primarily from experience. Most Indian architects who came to prominence in the 1950s and 1960s were less influenced by this tradition than the Rationalist.

FIRST GENERATION MODERNIST ARCHITECTURE

In the early days of post-Independence euphoria, it was Bauhaus rationalism that captured the hearts of many architects. Bauhaus paradigms were soon infiltrated by other ideas, some home-grown, some imported. The most important of these external influences was that of Frank Lloyd Wright. In many ways his impact on India was contemporaneous to that of the Gropius but he was soon on the back-burner.

The Empiricists: Frank Lloyd Wright and Beyond

Although some Indian architects are convinced that Frank Lloyd Wright made a brief visit to the Ramakrishna Mission in Calcutta seeking spiritual guidance, there is no hard evidence that he ever did so. It was through the apprenticeship system at Taliesen that he had any contact with Indian architects. It led to his one, unbuilt, design for India: the Calico Mills Administrative Office in Ahmedabad (1946). It was never executed because, according to Wright, the design demanded too much of Indian construction skills. According to another source, the clients, the Sarabhai family, and Wright were at loggerheads (Devane, 1996).

The influence of Frank Lloyd Wright's architecture is clear in the design of Chidambaram (1954), a house designed by Gira Sarabhai for Vikram and Mrinalini Sarabhai. Lying at the end of a curved driveway, the entrance is a double-heighted volume. The living areas sit to one side of the entrance and the service areas to the other. The handling of planes, cantilevered slabs, the contrast of stone and smooth walls and the integration of interior and exterior all show Wright's influence. What is achieved is an airy, livable house. George Nakashima designed the furniture in the living areas giving the overall design a further organic touch.

Although Joseph Allen Stein had little direct contact with Frank Lloyd Wright, his work of the 1950s (e.g., the India International Centre, 1959–62) and the early 1960s (e.g., the American International School, 1962–8) owes much to Wright's ideas. It is 'organic' in aesthetic character and strives for an alliance with nature eschewing the orthogonal geometries and abstract formal compositions of the Rationalists. Much of Stein's subsequent work such as the Ford Foundation Building (1969) and the UNICEF Building (1981) shows a continued consistency in a line of thought about architecture.

The Calico Mills Administration Building proposal, Ahmedabad

The India International Centre [IIC] is characterised by a flow of spaces linking various components of the complex through open passageways and inner and outer courts. The Centre consists of two wings; one offers residential accommodation, dining room and lounges overlooking the adjacent Lodi Gardens; the other is a public facilities wing. The latter consists of an auditorium, library, conference rooms and administrative facilities. A covered portico links the two wings and encloses a courtyard used for gatherings. An inner courtyard serves as an amphitheatre although it is today seldom used. As the building is now air-conditioned, the passages originally open, are enclosed. The complex has a horizontal emphasis with the stair-tower, as a vertical feature,

Chidambaram, Ahmedabad

The India International Centre, New Delhi

acting as a strong counterpoint. It is built of local stone and reinforced concrete, in-situ concrete frames and burnt clay jaalis. The dining room is roofed with a reinforced concrete lattice structure that spans the whole space. The complex succeeds in establishing a pleasant sequence of spaces in a manner that few institutional buildings manage.

The diversity of Empiricist work in India can be seen by comparing three very different buildings: the National Institute of Design (NID; 1961) in Ahmedabad designed by Gautam Sarabhai with inputs from Gira, the Kothari Building in Chennai (1961–3) designed by S.L. Chitale, and Mansinh M. Rana's Jawaharlal Nehru Memorial Library (1968) in the grounds of Teen Murti House in New Delhi. A fourth building illustrates the Empiricist philosophy in a very different building type; it is the Indian Express Building (1967–70) in Mumbai designed by Stein. What places buildings in the Empiricist tradition of design is a concern with what does and does not work in terms of everyday life.

The National Institute of Design, like Chidambaram, is clearly influenced by Frank Lloyd Wright although a decade had passed since the Sarabhais had been at Taliesen. The use of solid and void, the reinforced concrete framed structure with brick in-fill panels, the horizontal layering of the building, the manner of linking inside and outside, and the ties to nature all reflect Wright's organic architecture in other than geometric terms. The Sanskar Kendra designed by Le Corbusier a few years earlier in the city may well also have influenced the structural system of the NID. The NID's brick shell roof and pre-cast floor system were certainly highly innovative. The almost contemporaneous Kothari Building is, in contrast, simpler.

The Kothari Building is a six-storey framed structure on pile foundations. It has a typical office floor plan with a central lift core—a type closely tied to economic realities. The western and southern façades of the building have light

The National Institute of Design, Ahmedabad

The Indian Express Building, Mumbai

The Kothari Building, Chennai

louvres systems that are more effective than the *brise soleil* in providing protection from the sun. They are also, however, considerably less bold sculpturally. The trade-off between artistic expression and functionality is a decision all architects have to make. If it is fame that an architect seeks, the former is privileged.

A casual glance would suggest that the Kothari Building owes a debt to Marcel Breuer (1902–81), whose intellectual contribution to Chennai's Life Insurance Corporation [LIC] Building (1956–9) Chitale warmly acknowledges. Marcel Breuer was a Bauhaus-educated Modernist who had once (1937–40) been in partnership with Gropius. His influence on the LIC Building shows the diversity of inspirational sources for Indian architects. Certainly Breuer's attention to detail remains worthy of emulation.

Mansingh Rana, who worked for Wright at Taliesen from 1947 to 1951, has described his own work as 'organic, always evolving, never copying from the past, yet drawing from it' (M. Chatterjee, 1985). There are few better descriptions of the Empiricist attitude to design. The Jawaharlal Memorial Library is a two-storey structure designed with readers in mind. They have been provided with both good settings for reading and good views to the exterior. The entrance uses bold concrete forms with an interpenetration of horizontal and vertical forms while the remainder of the brick building is a more subdued backdrop—a ground for the figure of the entrance.

Much Empiricist architecture consists of low buildings. Designing skyscrapers so that they deal with local contexts is difficult. In one sense almost all high-rise office towers are variations of a single model: a service core surrounded by open subdividable space surrounded by a façade that lets light penetrate the interior while keeping out rain and unwanted sunlight. At the ground floor is the entrance lobby facing the street. The Indian Express Building is little different. In it, however, Stein made a valiant effort to address the basic requirements of orientation. The façades have been designed with the intensity of Indian light as much as with modernity of expression in mind. They are not dictated by overriding intellectual aesthetic demands but by the job at hand. This need in architecture may seem obvious but the contemporaneous Chatterjee International Tower in Calcutta had to have its entire façade replaced because of constructional problems (Majumdar, 2000).

The Rationalist architecture of the era stands in strong contrast to these buildings. Its visual clarity and the boldness of its expression in Europe and the Americas captured the imagination of many Indian architects. More simply, they accepted, at the beginning, at least, that it was *the* approach to architecture—that no other was acceptable.

European Rationalism and Beyond

The Bauhaus masters developed an architecture that they thought was style free. A pattern did, however, emerge. The buildings had Cubist forms, flat roofs and façades, little or no embellishment, and windows capped by shades. They turned their backs (or sides) to streets and, in mass housing design, they were arranged slab by slab in rows, around large open spaces, or as point towers in grassed areas. The overriding design criterion was that adequate sunlight was to penetrate all the rooms. Emphasis was placed on organising the plans to ensure efficiency of movement; the construction methods also emphasised efficiency. Like all caricatures, this description is unfair because regional factors did exert an influence. Nevertheless, designs of a similar nature were built from the Arctic to the Tropics, and in all cultures.

Rationalist architecture gave India aesthetically simple designs, large buildings, point skyscrapers and slab blocks all harnessing modern technology. The widespread use of flat roofs and simple horizontal lines and fenestration suggests that architects working in India kept up-to-date with contemporary European Rationalist concepts of architecture. Buildings such as rest and circuit houses and even industrial buildings such as power stations (e.g., the Indraprastha Power Station in Delhi) have, in retrospect, a surprisingly modern appearance.

Forgotten works of modern architecture abound in India but the first by an Indian architect to which can be attributed a significant new way of thinking is probably West Bengal's New Secretariat (1949–54) designed by Habib Rahman. He had returned to India from America 'full of Gropius, Oscar Niemeyer (b.1907) and Brazil' (Rahman, 1988). The Gandhi Ghat Memorial in Barrackpur (1948) was actually Rahman's first completed work but it is the New Secretariat that shows the impact of his American training. The memorial is an exploration of structural ideas and architectural symbolism. It consists of a tower in a simplified temple *shikhara* form, a horizontal cantilevered slab below which is a non-structural mushroom column. It represents not only an architect's structural dexterity but also Gandhi's respect for all religions. The Secretariat is a fifteen storey Modernist building showing the clarity of form sought by the Bauhaus while exploring the juxtaposition of geometric forms, and vertical and horizontal lines. Pigeonhole shades keep the sun off the southern façade.

Rahman was not alone. The work of Achyut Kanvinde shows enthusiasms similar to his. Kanvinde's designs for the Ahmedabad Textile Industry's Research Association [ATIRA] Building (1950–2) and the first phase of the Physical Research Laboratory [PRL] (1953–4), both in Ahmedabad, show the clear imprint of the Bauhaus. His design for the National Botanical Research Institute (1957; very like the Bauhaus building in Weimar), residential hostels for the King George's Medical College (1960–70) and the Toxology Research Centre (1969–70), all in Lucknow, show the same influence. While Kanvinde is still proud of his Ahmedabad work, he believes his Lucknow designs to be of less interest (Kanvinde, 2000). He is probably over-critical of it.

Another contemporary work, the Intercontinental (now Oberoi) Hotel (1958) in New Delhi by Durga Bajpai and Piloo Mody is clearly in the International style promulgated by Gropius. In contrast to the Intercontinental, one finds various

The ATIRA Building, Ahmedabad

The Intercontinental [now Oberoi] Hotel, New Delhi

other Modernist influences in their remaining work. The Jahangir Art Gallery (1952–3) in Mumbai has a plasticity of form akin to the work of Eero Saarinen (1900–61). The spirit of Bajpai's *oeuvre* also reflects that of Alvar Aaalto for whom he once worked. Aalto's attitudes are perhaps most clearly reflected in Bajpai's design for the Tata Institute of Social Sciences (1951–4) in Mumbai. Its exuberance and its relationship to Mumbai's climate exemplify Aalto's willingness to experiment (Correa, 2000). At the same time it is considerably more Empiricist in character than Bajpai's later work.

The ideas of Gropius and the Bauhaus, as presented in their North American context, were far from simply aped in India. Gropius' design philosophy, not necessarily his forms, and its application in India is most clearly evident in Kanvinde's designs of the ATIRA and the PRL buildings. The functional areas in both buildings are separated although linked; they both have a purity of form and they both use newly developed building technologies. The ATIRA building has open plan, zoned activity areas, and its administration-cum-laboratory component is in a rectangular form. The sunshades on the southern façade run the full course of the building in continuous lines while on the northern façade the fenestration is flush with the wall. In these buildings, Kanvinde introduced the flexible concrete column and beam grid to India. In the Bank of India Building (1961) in Bhadra, Ahmedabad, he pioneered the use of the waffle slab.

These architectural, structural and constructional ideas were all highly influential in India simply because their logic and utility were easy to understand and follow. The appropriateness to India of this early work remains a question. Kanvinde's work of the era has certainly held up, intellectually and physically, remarkably well over time. His effort, following his client's wishes, to symbolically Indianise his work of the period is exemplified by his design for the Azad Bhavan (1958–61) in New Delhi. The treatment there is, however, superficial and it was only after the influential seminars on the nature of architecture for India at the Lalit Kala Akademi that Kanvinde really became his own person (Panchal, 1998).

The Bauhaus influence also ran through Habib Rahman's PWD work in New Delhi until the end of the 1950s. After that his designs, still Modernist, reflected more his own identity. Rahman was Senior Architect (1953–70) and later Chief Architect (1970–4) of the CPWD in New Delhi. In these roles he was responsible for much of the work that gives central New Delhi its character to this day. These buildings include Dak Tar Bhavan (1954; the Post and Telegraph Building), the Auditor and General Controller's office (1958), the Indraprastha Bhavan (1965), the World Health Organization Building (1963), the Curzon Road Hostel (1967), the multi-storey flats at Ramakrishnapuram (1965) and Patel Bhavan (1972–3). It was in the design of Rabindra Bhavan (1961) that Rahman's own architectural development showed a breaking away from a direct repetition of Bauhaus thinking. He was aided in making this break by Nehru (see 'Tribute Habib Rahman', 1996).

Rahman's first design for the Rabindra Bhavan was a box-like Bauhaus-inspired effort considered to be 'nonsense' by Nehru when he examined the proposal. Rahman redesigned the building into a more free-flowing form with slender, continuous chajjas and jaalis in abstract rather than literal forms. (Rahman, 1988, 1994). Both these elements have a Modernist quality to them so their incorporation did little to dilute the idiom of the design whereas chhattris would have done so. Yet Rahman was not averse to using historical models. In the design of the Mazars of Maulana Azad (1960) and President Fakhruddin Ali Ahmed (1975), Rahman used traditional forms as the basis for his designs in what is now regarded as a post-Modern manner.

Contemporaneous with Rahman's early work in Delhi was that of another influential figure in Indian architecture, Cyrus S.H. Jhabvala. His design for Kirorimal College (1954–6) at Delhi University has more in common with the

Azad Bhavan, New Delhi

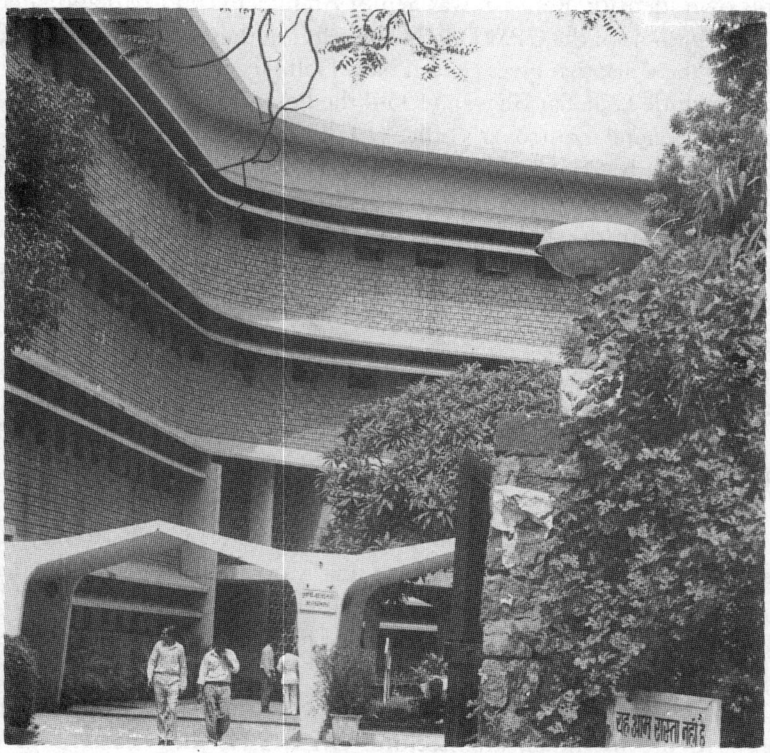

Rabindra Bhavan, New Delhi

subdued Modernist architecture of the Scandinavian countries than the Bauhaus. The college has a linear organisation with an entrance lobby that opens up on to a canopied spine. Classrooms are linked to this spine through courtyards on one side and to the administration unit and library on the other (M. Chatterjee, 1985). In presentation, the building has a simple geometry based on a grid system.

This simplicity of form is also a hallmark of the work of Vanu Bhuta at the Gandhi Smarak (1956), Rajghat, Delhi and of Charles Correa in his design for the Gandhi Smarak Sangrahalaya (1958–63) in Ahmedabad. Bhuta's is a simple design. Correa's in Ahmedabad is more complex. His design shows the link between a number of Modernist artistic ideas and Gandhian philosophy, especially in the frugality of the means used to achieve architectural ends. The unheroic nature of the grid of pyramidal roofs, the patterns of light and shade and the openness of plan remain an exemplary marriage of function and form in much more than the strict Modernist sense of activity and container—of designing a space or room simply to allow an activity to be carried out efficiently. It is as successful a homage to Gandhi as is Rahman's Barrackpur memorial and Bhuta's Gandhi Smarak. The goals of the three designers and the mechanisms they used differed, even though each was influenced by Gropius. These three designs show the originality and variety of Indian interpretations of Modernist ideals.

Hasmukh Patel is another architect whose work can be included in this first generation of architects although he is younger and his work came later. Studying at Cornell he was less heavily influenced by Gropius than others of his architectural generation. The precision of his work reflects Mies van der Rohe, although his architecture does not. Another modernist whose education (at McGill in Montreal) was distant from the immediate effect of the Bauhaus was Bennett Pithavadian.

As Pithavadian's practice was located in Chennai, outside the major architectural circles of contemporary India, his work is also less known. Modern architecture in southern India tended to follow its own course anyway because fewer architects from the region had much opportunity to study abroad. Pithavadian believed that the spatial forms of International Modernism were largely irrelevant in India. What makes him a Modernist, nevertheless, is that he absorbed the intellectual position of the Modernists, including that of Gropius, but not necessarily the stylistic devices of so-called functionalism. His work shows the blending of Rationalist and Empiricist approaches that became more prevalent in India twenty years later.

Pithavadian's functionalism was based on what the realities of India were, not what they should be. He ascribed this position to John Bland at McGill who believed that architecture should be based on an 'empathetic relationship' between client and architect with the structure of a building being the generator of its form (Pithavadian, 1984,1988). The Home Science Block (1952–4) of the Women's Christian College and the Indian Overseas Bank (1962) both in Chennai, illustrate Pithavadian's early work. The Modernist ideology shows through in his effort

The Gandhi Smarak Sangrahalaya, Ahmedabad

The Gandhi Smarak, Delhi

The Indian Overseas Bank, Chennai

to relate form to function. The Empirical nature of Pithavadian's work is demonstrated by his concern for how India and its buildings function. The module for the Home Sciences Block is 8 foot 3 inches [2515 mm] to meet the requirements of a science laboratory; for the bank building it is a 4 foot [1220 mm] grid to meet the requirements of an office building. In both cases, Pithavadian recognised that the buildings would have to operate in an environment of heat and dust, poor maintenance and poor cleaning, especially of latrines. In both buildings there is an openness of plan—a fundamental tenet of Modernism—and the use of vertical louvres to provide shading from the sun without catching dust. Pithavadian also recognised the limits of the workmanship available to him in construction.

Despite these variations from the central themes of International Modernism, it was the work of Gropius and the International Style that exerted the strongest influence on modern architecture in India until the impact of Le Corbusier began to be felt on a widespread basis in the 1960s. Indeed, Gropius's tenets still continue to underlie much work worldwide. They were based on a clear logic that made, and still makes, considerable sense in its appropriate context.

A REFLECTION

It is not surprising that Indian architects have turned to the experiences of others in addressing their own problems. Architectural thinking in the United States of

America was totally dominated by British and Continental European architectural ideas from the earliest days of colonisation until the work of Louis Sullivan (1856–1924) and Frank Lloyd Wright began to have an impact. Even then, Art Deco, although adapted to its sub-tropical context in places such as Miami Beach, was a European import. Today, Deconstructionist thought in America is largely, if not entirely, European in origin. These observations do not mean that architecture in the United States has not developed its own character nor that it has made no contributions to European architecture; it means that much can be learnt from experiences everywhere.

The work of the first generation of post-Independence Modernist architects in India had a profound effect on what followed. This effect has to be seen in the context of its times. The architecture of the British was politically unacceptable even if its slow three-centuries-long adaptation to regional climates of India was grudgingly admired (Jain, 1991). In contrast to what Batley offered, the Modernists of the first generation sought a complete break from the past and a new vision for the future. Nevertheless, Batley's presence, often hidden, continues to be felt on the Indian scene.

Other architects and mistris soon picked up the patterns of form that the first generation of Modernists in India introduced. Buildings started to be massed horizontally with plinths closer to the ground. Large glass windows in horizontal bands, freestanding staircases and cantilevered porches began to appear in many buildings, even factories and power stations. In domestic architecture, living rooms and dining rooms became one space (although often the latter retained its place as the fulcrum of a house) and in houses for the wealthy, bathrooms became attached to bedrooms. Much to the delight of Portland cement manufacturers, reinforced concrete structures and flat concrete roofs, even when inappropriate climatically, became *the* hallmark of a modern building everywhere in India. India was thus ready for the arrival of Le Corbusier. He built on the willingness of Indian architects to explore new ideas and he also provided a different vision of what architecture should be.

4

The Second Generation: 1950 to 1980

THE DISTINCTION between the first and second generation of Modernist architecture depends on the nature of the buildings designed and, particularly, on the sources of their architects' inspirations. It is only partly a matter of chronology. Much of the work of both generations coexisted with that of the Batley generation in time and, in most cities, space. Individual architects too could be identified with different generations at different phases in their careers. The work of a number of the architects of the first generation matured and changed significantly as architectural theory throughout the world evolved. Many of the buildings they designed during a new phase of their careers are part of the body of second generation work described here.

If the architects of first generation Modernist work generally found their inspirations by going out of India to be absorbed in the ideas of Walter Gropius or Frank Lloyd Wright, the second generation found their inspiration in the work of a wider array of international masters. Le Corbusier, a Rationalist, and Louis I. Kahn, more of an Empiricist, were particularly important because of their direct contact with India. Of the pair, Le Corbusier was the more influential because of his greater involvement in the country as an architect, an employer and as an author of polemical writings. Louis Kahn came to India later and executed only one project in the country. He was, however, the educator of a number of people who later became influential in Indian architectural circles.

A third influence came from changes that occurred in the education of architects. Influential international architects, advising or working in conjunction with Indian innovators, directed these changes. Of these visitors Charles Eames (1907–78) and Ray Eames (1912–88) had major international standing. Their influence on architecture was largely indirect because it had an impact via the educational system for young product designers. In particular it pushed aside for three decades at least, for better or worse, both the architectural focus and the pedagogical methods of Claude Batley at the Sir J.J. School in Mumbai.

The Entrance, the Assembly Hall (Legislature), Chandigarh

A fourth influence came from those architects and engineers who explored the architecture of structural possibilities, something that coincided with the historically strong engineering influence on architecture in India. As elsewhere, there were architectural experiments in the country with folded slabs, hyperbolic-paraboloid shells and lightweight structures. The international masters in structural innovation who exerted an influence throughout the world during the 1960s and 1970s included Robert Maillart (1872–1940), Pier Luigi Nervi (1891–1979) and Felix Candela (1910–97).

The work of the homegrown architects of the first generation, particularly Correa and Kanvinde, was another influence on the generation of architecture that followed it. Nevertheless, it was the presence of Le Corbusier that transformed Modernist architecture in India for the next two decades.

LE CORBUSIER

Le Corbusier was Swiss born and raised within Calvinism, a parsimonious and ascetic Christian faith. After a two-decade long meandering exploration of architectural possibilities, he had established himself by 1950 as the archetypical artist-architect in Paris where he had lived since 1916. Despite his claims to the contrary, he had been a ferocious reader and had travelled widely. His ideas and architecture owe much to a number of sources: nineteenth century French Rationalist and utopian thinking, cubism in art, and elements drawn from his own studies in the Mediterranean (Brooks, 1997). By the time he came to India his work had moved away from the geometric simplicity of his purist phase—when the nature of the buildings he designed were akin to that of the International style of the Bauhaus—to a phase in which he used more rugged sculptural forms. Like architectural Rationalists in Italy he was particularly concerned with the juxtaposition of pure forms: the cylinder, cone and cube.

Le Corbusier's works and writings on architecture and urban design were well-known, if largely dismissed, in India during the 1930s and 1940s but became inspirational to many architects after his direct association with the country began. In 1950 he was hired along with his cousin Pierre Jeanneret (1896–1967) and the British husband-wife team of Maxwell Fry (1899–1987) and Jane Drew (1911–96) to design Chandigarh. His work there and later in Ahmedabad added a whole new dimension to the Indian architectural experience. It remains a revelation and serves as an evangelical message to many architects. It is also clear that his international reputation would have been substantially lower if it had not had been for the buildings he designed in Chandigarh and Ahmedabad.

Chandigarh

Chandigarh owes its existence to the partitioning of the Indian subcontinent in 1947; Lahore, Punjab's capital, became part of Pakistan and the eastern half of

Punjab in India needed a new one. Jawaharlal Nehru wanted the capital of India's Punjab to be designed by a significant modern architect. A plan and some preliminary ideas for the government complex were developed by Albert Mayer (1897–1981) of New York and Mathew Nowicki (1910–51), a Polish architect teaching in North Carolina (Mayer, 1950; Mumford, 1954). After Nowicki's death in an aeroplane crash and Mayer's lack of interest in pursuing the project, a new architectural team was sought. P.N. Thapar, the Chief Administrator of the project and P.L. Varma, Punjab's Chief Engineer, went to Europe to select an architect, with a list of major Modernists in hand. They chose Le Corbusier. With some cajoling by the Indian ambassador to France, H. Malik, and France's Minister of Culture, André Malraux, and at the insistence of Fry and Drew, he agreed to be involved. Not everybody was happy that another set of outsiders was to design a major work in India. It was felt that competent Indian architects were available and should have been selected for the job (Grover, 1996).

The plan of Chandigarh (1952) is a rationalisation and 'de-Anglo-Saxonisation' of that developed by Mayer and Nowicki. Le Corbusier straightened the road and park network designed by them to follow contours and watercourses into a 'rational' orthogonal grid. Chandigarh is a low-rise *Ville Radieuse* (Le Corbusier, 1961). Le Corbusier kept for himself the design of the capital complex and, at least partially, some other major buildings—a museum and an exhibition hall, constructed in 1964–86 (Bahga, Bahga and Bahga, 1993). The housing designs were allocated to Fry and Drew, Jeanneret and others. The work of the Indian architects who followed Le Corbusier—the Chandigarh School—used his geometric principles so closely that it is not always possible to distinguish between the work done by Le Corbusier and what is the work of his disciples.

The capital complex is a Modernist version of Lutyen's New Delhi (Evenson, 1966; Nilsson 1973; Kalia 1987). The complex in New Delhi is organised around a major axial road, the Rajpath, but Chandigarh, truly Modernist, turns its back

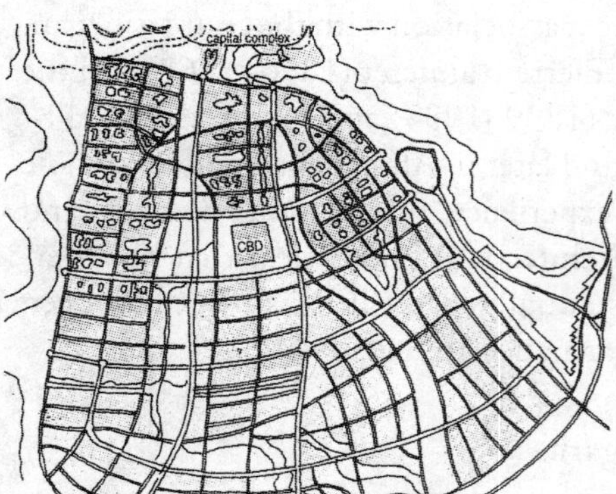

Chandigarh: The Mayer-Nowicki plan

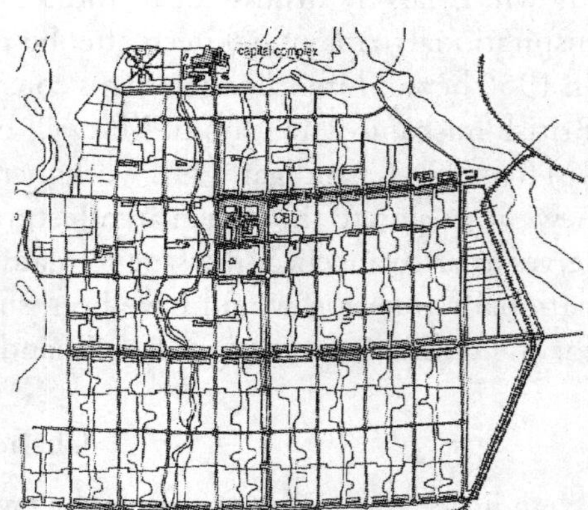

Chandigarh: The Le Corbusier plan

on the streets and is organised around a major pedestrian plaza. Impressive in size, but largely devoid of life, the plaza consists of the Palace of Ministers (i.e., the Secretariat), the Assembly Hall, the Palace of the Governor (yet to be built), the High Court and the Palace of the Winds. The Open Hand is a symbolic feature of the group. Unlike New Delhi, it is the Secretariat not the Assembly Hall that is in the background. Looking at the scheme from the city approach (i.e., from the south), the Governor's Palace is at the head, the High Court on the right and the Assembly Hall on the left, symbolising the three centres of government. The Open Hand is to the right front and the Palace of the Winds close in on the left side. The Secretariat is relegated to the rear of the Assembly Hall.

The architecture itself is based on ideas Le Corbusier had proposed for a number of earlier projects (e.g., the League of Nations in 1927 and the 1949 project for the United Nations in New York). The complex forms a bold scheme of abstract forms that enthrals visiting architects, and gives many Indians, especially the residents of Chandigarh, a sense of pride. Nehru said he thought the High Court was 'grand' and the Secretariat 'magnificent' (Prasad, 1987).

Concrete was the major building material used. Its employment affords dramatic roof forms, bold sculptural and vertical elements and the *brise soleil.* Standard building components—rainwater spouts, ramps, and balusters—become celebrated features. Bright primary colours for doors and windows stand in strong contrast to the grey of the concrete. Above all, the use of the parasol shell form on *pilotes,* the interpenetration of spaces, solids and voids, and shadow and light, were all new to twentieth century India (V. Prakash, 1999). There are a number of Indian referents in the architecture of the buildings (e.g., the roof of the Assembly Hall has the curve of a cow's horns). Some critics see close links between the overall site layout of the capital complex and the broken symmetries of the hierarchical set of spaces at Fatehpur Sikri. It is, however, the startlingly new combination of features in the city that made many Indian architects, like their compatriots everywhere, as Nehru said, 'sit up and think'.

The City Centre in Sector 17 best exemplifies the architectural 'type' of Chandigarh. The layout of the complex, like that of the capital complex, is based on the super-block schema with vehicular traffic kept to the periphery and a pedestrianised area in the centre. The open plan buildings, the use of concrete column and slab and, often, concrete walls, the way the walls are set back to afford balconies, and the broken symmetries in formal organisation are all hallmarks of Le Corbusier's work.

Like Lutyens in New Delhi, Le Corbusier achieved a sense of architectural monumentality in Chandigarh. At Bhubaneswar the goal was to break down caste and socio-economic barriers through the location of housing types; the sectors of Chandigarh on the contrary, are socio-economically segregated. The socio-economic status of each of the 1,000 metre by 800 metre sectors is clear to the residents of the city and it is not long before even the most casual of visitors recognises it. A longitudinal park runs through each sector and a bazaar street cuts across

Chandigarh: The Capital Complex

Chandigarh: The City Centre

it at its centre. As at Bhubaneswar, the sector is an applied version of the generic neighbourhood unit idea.

All the architects involved in Chandigarh worried about dealing appropriately with the Indian climate and construction techniques (including the use of labour intensive building methods). The housing designs show a variety of innovations. Jeanneret's use of an interplay of decorative brickwork and plain plaster to make his buildings look grander than they really are was new to India and Fry and Drew introduced the Le Corbusian egg-crate *brise-soleil* into domestic work. Even as it addresses the Indian context, the city nevertheless remains international in character (Evenson, 1966; Kalia, 1987; Joshi, 1999). Perhaps the most telling comment on Chandigarh is that of a disciple, Balkrishna V. Doshi (b.1927): Chandigarh 'gives us Le Corbusier's sense of the future not [a present] Indian life.' The impact of the Ahmedabad projects was similar.

Ahmedabad

Le Corbusier designed three villas, Villa Shodhan (1954), Sarabhai House (1955) and the unbuilt Chinubhai House, for wealthy mill-owning families. Two institutional buildings, the Millowners' Association Headquarters (1954–6) and the Sanskar Kendra (1957), a museum, were also designed by him.

Villa Shodhan is a cubical concrete structure with a separate kitchen block. The design for the Chinubhai house was similar while the Sarabhai House is a low-profiled, ground-hugging building. The design of Villa Shodhan has antecedents in Le Corbusier's explorations of the 1920s in houses such as the Maison Citrohan. The house's flat roof is separated from its walls by a continuous band of windows. The cube is penetrated either by large glass windows which afford views of the garden or by tiny slits to allow light into the interior. The ground floor consists of double storey reception rooms and a ramp that gives access to the floors above. Three bedroom suites open onto the first floor terrace. In contrast to Villa Shodhan's cubical form, the Sarabhai House is a horizontal building in which the interior and exterior flow into each other.

In form, the Millowners' Association Building consists of a number of additions to and subtractions from a cube as in Le Corbusier's earlier Villa Cook (1926). The building has a bold western front dominated by a *brise-soleil* and an approach ramp with a freestanding staircase as a sculptural work set apart from the façade. Internally, the penetration of spaces and the play of light and shade add to the overall sculptural effect of the building. The building serves little instrumental purpose now, something that until very recently, was also true of the Sanskar Kendra.

The museum is a pure rectangular form standing on pylons much like Le Corbusier's museum in Chandigarh. It is concrete-framed with brick in-fill panels. Internally its design is based on a square spiral; the entry is by a ramp that leads from the ground floor to the central core of the first floor. Until the middle

The Shodhan House, Ahmedabad

The Sarabhai House, Ahmedabad

of 2000 the building stood largely vacant. Happily, it now houses a permanent exhibition on the city of Ahmedabad. Plenty of room remains for the exhibition's expansion!

In looking at the work of a foreign architect, the question almost inevitably

The Millowners' Association Headquarters, Ahmedabad

arises: 'What does it have to do with us?' Le Corbusier said he wished to create an architecture for 'India of the second half of the twentieth century' (Prasad, 1987). To some commentators, his architecture is an abstraction of traditional Indian patterns of design (Correa, 1984; Curtis, 1985). These associations are largely coincidental for Le Corbusier had framed his compositional ideas long before coming to India. They do, however, show the universality of many of the concerns that architects address. What Le Corbusier learnt from India was that the texture and richness of concrete could be exploited sculpturally in the hands of relatively low-skilled workers (M. Chatterjee, 1985).

The Impact of Le Corbusier and the Chandigarh Architects

Le Corbusier's Indian followers loved his futurist thinking—his unequivocal and boldly stated vision of what architecture (and cities) should be. His impact has occurred in four phases. During the first honeymoon phase his work was almost directly copied. During the second his ideas appeared to be more important than his forms. During the third his work was disparaged and all its faults and irrelevancies were pointed out. Now his work is being assessed anew for what it affords India.

The first phase of Le Corbusier's influence on India is not surprising for many young architects had developed close connections with him. Certainly, his presentation of himself as an individual creative genius impressed young Indian architects, particularly northwestern Indian architects. The east and south largely escaped his influence. Many young architects worked for him either in Chandigarh or on his Ahmedabad buildings. The list is impressive in terms of their subsequent contribution to the architecture of India and to the profession. The roll includes Jughal Kishore Chowdhury (b.1918), Aditya Prakash (b.1921), Jeet Lal Malhotra (b.1929), Arvind Jayantilal Talati (b.1930) and Jasbir Sachdev (b.1931). B.V. Doshi worked for Le Corbusier in Paris, then was his site architect in Chandigarh (1954–7) and was deeply involved in Le Corbusier's Ahmedabad work.

Many of the architects who worked for Le Corbusier executed work using his design patterns. Some became locked into it stylistically but others, such as Doshi, while owing a long-lasting debt to Le Corbusier, evolved very much into their own people. As Doshi put it: young architects 'learnt from him how to look at structure and functions . . . how to create space from elements . . . to achieve a form in relation to the landscape around it' (Curtis, 1988).

Le Corbusier's international colleagues were also influential even if to a much lesser extent. Of them, Jeanneret worked in India the longest, from 1951 to 1965. With a deep concern for India, he made a lasting impact on the people with whom he worked. Apart from the housing work, in Chandigarh he was involved in the site planning for Punjab University and designed the Gandhi Bhavan (1959–61) there (Joshi, 1999). Maxwell Fry took over the project to design the Life Insurance Corporation Building (1957) in Calcutta from Durga Bajpai but Mody and Colgan of Mumbai later completed it. Jane Drew worked tirelessly for Chandigarh to be recognised as a World Heritage Site and thus constantly kept the city in the world's as well as architects' eyes.

The indirect impact of Le Corbusier's work via the work of other architects can also be seen in India. Indian architects of the era were inspired by the extensive Le Corbusier-inspired Modernist work built in Brazil while Europe was at war. There are specific buildings by Brazilian architects like Oscar Niemeyer that have counterparts in India. Among the best known of such buildings is the Apsara Cinema (c.1968) in Mumbai designed by Yahya Merchant which has direct formal antecedents in Niemeyer's work, probably his Chapel of San Francisco in Pampulha (Lang, Desai and Desai, 1997). It is, however, the *idea* of Brazil and its architectural achievements that was probably more of an inspiration.

Le Corbusier's impact on India was thus at many levels—as an employer, as a theorist, as a form giver and as an educator. A decade later others responded to Louis Kahn in much the same manner as to Le Corbusier. Although admiring Le Corbusier and his work, Kahn came from a very different intellectual tradition.

LOUIS I. KAHN

Louis I. Kahn, born in Estonia and raised in Philadelphia, received a classical Beaux-Arts architectural education and later attended the American Academy in

Rome. His knowledge of the classical tradition shaped his architecture life-long. He is perhaps best known for his concern for the nature of materials and how surfaces can be formed to frame light. He spoke of architecture poetically in a way that captures the imagination. Kahn arrived in India at his creative peak while he was still working out many of his ideas. He learnt much from his experiences in India and what he learnt is reflected in his final works.

Kahn had been selected from a short list of international architects apparently compiled by Gautam and Gira Sarabhai to design the Indian Institute of Management [IIM] in Ahmedabad. The goal was to attain immediate international recognition for the institution through its architecture. Although Kahn completed only that one major project in India, he designed two other important building complexes in South Asia that are sources of considerable commentary. These designs were for the Sher-E-Banglanagar National Capital (1963–4), the legislative capital for Pakistan in Dhaka in what is now Bangladesh, and the site plan and estate of the President of Pakistan (1963–5) in Islamabad. He also did some very preliminary sketch designs for Gandhinagar (1963–4), and designed a family planning centre (1970–4) in Kathmandu, Nepal that was only partially built.

At the IIM, Kahn created an austere set of geometrically organised buildings that form shaded courts. These courts vary in size to provide a variety of settings and experiences. The brick walls rise unrelieved. They shed their load in great arches—segmental, relieving or full. While monumental in a homely way, the sequential experience provided by moving through the buildings and the subsequent opening and closing of vistas give a humane scale to the complex. Kahn's use of brick had an impact on India (and many other places) as did his orchestration of a composition of open spaces and buildings.

Kahn's influence occurred in much the same way as Le Corbusier's but on a smaller scale. He wrote less about his work and claimed less for it than Le Corbusier did for his own ideas and work. Those architects who worked for Kahn—people such as Doshi, Anant Raje (b.1929), Kulbushan Jain (b.1940) and Chandra Sen Kapadia (b.1936)—held him and his thought processes in high esteem and learnt much from him. They largely mediated his influence on Indian architects.

Doshi and Raje, then working together, acted as liaison officers for Kahn with the local business community, the sponsors of the IIM project. Doshi acted as the site architect for Kahn and, as in the case of his earlier work for Le Corbusier, a number of his suggestions were incorporated into the design. Raje subsequently spent five years (1964–9) working in Kahn's Philadelphia office and although he took over the design of the IIM after Kahn's death in 1974, he did not work on the IIM project in Philadelphia.

Kahn, like Le Corbusier, had a formal architectural vocabulary that was attractive to and emulated by many architects. His use of scale showed architects that one did not have to be monumental to be seen. What Kahn does is to explore

The Indian Institute of Management, Ahmedabad

the use of brick, a material familiar to Indian builders, in his South Asian work. His use of load-bearing exposed brick construction and the use of arches and circular openings became part of the structural and aesthetic vocabulary of later architects of the subcontinent.

Kahn also made an important contribution to education when Doshi was setting up the School of Architecture at the Centre for Environmental Planning and Technology [CEPT] in Ahmedabad. Bernard Kohn, who, with Doshi, was the first co-director of the architectural course, was a former student of Kahn's in his Master Class at the University of Pennsylvania. During the 1970s, the School of Architecture at CEPT was highly influential in setting both architectural and educational trends in northern India. Another institution in Ahmedabad, the National Institute of Design, was equally influential but in a different manner.

THE NATIONAL INSTITUTE OF DESIGN

In 1958, Ray and Charles Eames prepared a report, the *Eames Report* (known in their writings as *The India Report*) that served as the manifesto for the educational processes developed at the National Institute for Design [NID] in Ahmedabad (Eames and Eames, 1967). Indirectly, it steered the brief and thus the design of the building itself (Kirkham, 1995). The Eameses are better known as furniture designers than architects although their own house has been widely published. Indeed, the possession of a Charles Eames lounge chair with matching footstool was a status symbol in India during the 1960s. Important though their furniture designs are, it is the curriculum design for the NID which is of interest here. While not generally recognised, the impact of the curriculum at the NID on architectural education has been substantial.

In their report the Eameses note that the major impact on Indian design was not some influence from the West or East but the 'phenomenon of communication . . . that affects a world not a country.' The same statement could easily be made today, forty years later, and still seem erudite. Their message was a Modernist one: 'security lies in change'. They noted: 'India has a tradition and philosophy familiar with the meaning of creative destruction' and that in designing too there is the need to 'shut out all preconceived ideas about a subject and then to consider factor by factor.' They advocated a problem solving process rather than a process of mimesis as the basis for design thinking and they advocated the creation of a new institute and new approaches to teaching in India (Eames and Eames, 1967). Both came to fruition in the form of the NID.

The NID was formed to teach visual communication methods and product design, including interior design and architecture, although it is now more narrowly focused on design. For the staff, professional practice was regarded as continuing education and research. In 1964, the NID produced decorative themes for the New York World's Fair and again in 1967 in Montreal. With consultants, in the early 1960s, the NID designed an office building (Enrico Peressutti [1908–73], consultant), residential quarters (Harry Weese, consultant) and schemes such as the Indian Pavilion at the 1970 Osaka World's Fair (Frei Otto [b.1929], consultant). The NID is actually the architect of record for the IIM in Ahmedabad. Louis Kahn was officially the consultant. In architecture, the educational process at the NID worked primarily through trial and error within the studio system—something that has remained unchanged over the years. What did change was the introductory course.

The major curricula change in architectural schools as a consequence of the *Eames Report* was in the approach to design. From being based on composition, focus shifted to design as expression. Former students of Gropius and the Bauhaus masters had already initiated this change. It was founded on the Basic Design course developed at the Bauhaus by a small group of artists, primarily Johannes Itten, Paul Klee and Wassily Kandinsky (Itten, 1965). In India, from the 1960s onwards, the course replaced those on architectural composition as promoted by Claude Batley. Bennett Pithavadian, for instance, introduced it at what is now the Anna School in Chennai in 1964.

The study of the principles of Indian architecture got lost in the shuffle. That was not what the Eames had in mind. The results of the shift from theories of composition to Basic Design have been less successful in architecture than in art. The abandonment of concerns for order, rhythm and proportion in favour of free forms expressing an architect's feelings has often resulted in buildings competing for attention rather than complementing each other. The universal process of perception supposedly underlying the course is now known to be simply the highly creative invention by a few artists of one way of representing the world. It is an alternative system with its own rules, never clearly articulated, and recognised only by those who possess the 'right stuff' (see Wolfe, 1981).

A surprisingly small web of people were responsible for establishing the architectural debate in Ahmedabad in the 1960s and a new generation of Modernist work came from the ferment they created. With the designs of Rahman, Kanvinde, Correa, Le Corbusier and Kahn, a substantial body of new work existed in India. It was there to be seen and discussed and to be emulated or not.

THE SECOND GENERATION OF INDIAN MODERNIST ARCHITECTURE

The second generation of post-independence architecture differed in a number of ways from the first. The rationalism of Gropius gave way to the rationalism of Le Corbusier as the major influence but Gropius remained important as an architectural philosopher. In much the same way the empiricism of Frank Lloyd Wright gave way to that of Kahn. As time passed, the empiricism of Kahn yielded to that of a more diffuse set of pacesetters. Kahn and Frank Lloyd Wright nevertheless remained important role models.

The Rationalists

The influence of Le Corbusier is clearly evident in many buildings completed in India between 1960 and 1980. During the early part of that period—the first phase of his impact—the work of his followers was highly derivative but it evolved into a second phase in which his ideas were more evident than his forms. According to one careful observer, Malay Chatterjee, much of the work is forgettable (M. Chatterjee, 1985). This comment is harsh but it was not until architects began to address their local context that architecture in India began to have its own character.

The direct descendent of Chandigarh is Gandhinagar, the capital of the state of Gujarat which was necessary to build as the result of the bifurcation of Bombay state into Gujarat and Maharashtra in 1960. The city is based on the same intellectual model as Chandigarh and on a similar rational grid plan. While there are some important differences between the two plans, the two are cut from the same cloth.

Gandhinagar is located on the Sabarmati River upstream from Ahmedabad. Directed by Hargovind K. Medwa, the design of the city by the Gujarat PWD is based on the Chandigarh rectangular grid system, but with the capital complex at its heart not head. The architecture of the capital complex is large scale and attempts to follow the patterns of the Chandigarh buildings.

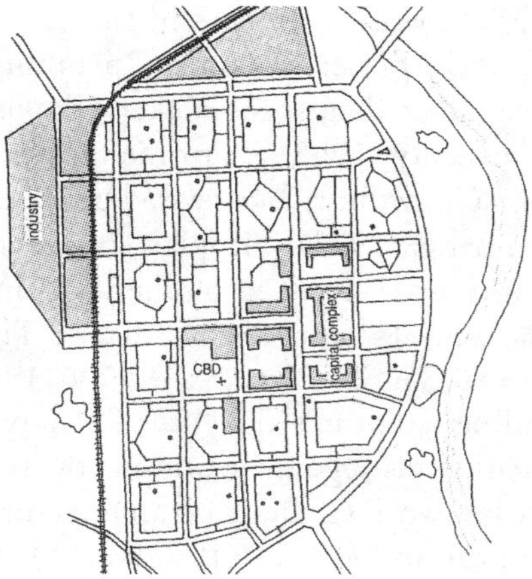

The Gandhinagar plan

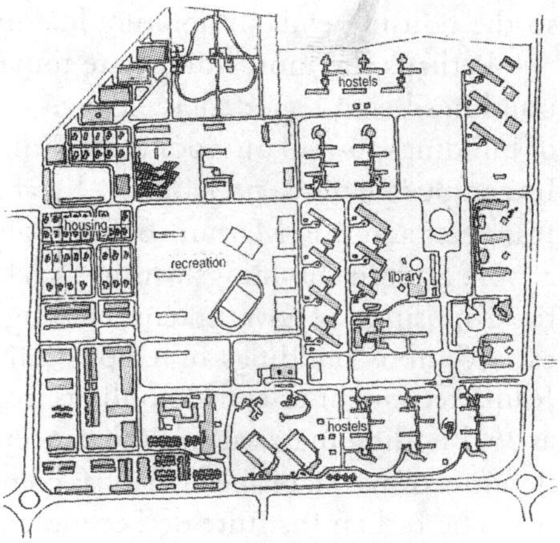

The Punjab University, Chandigarh, plan

The Gandhi Bhavan, Punjab University

The residential sectors house about 7,000 people each. Like Bhubaneswar and Chandigarh they are based on the neighbourhood unit concept. Each has schools, shopping areas, playgrounds and large parks. The mix of plotted and social housing affords some diversity in each residential area. An additional design goal was to create communities similar to those of the close-knit social and physical fabric of the *pols* of Ahmedabad (Gujarat State PWD, undated). The social nature of the pols is, however, impossible to recreate by fiat and the architectural layout of the residential areas in Gandhinagar has been rationalised into rectangular forms so the housing ends up looking like much PWD work elsewhere in India.

Perhaps the most immediate impact of Le Corbusier was on site-planning, buildings being regarded as elements in space rather than space-makers, the use of buildings to wall outdoor areas. Punjab University (1955) is a prime example. Its campus plan was prepared by Jugal Kishore Chowdhury but revised by Pierre Jeanneret and B.P. Mathur (Bahga, Bahga and Bahga, 1993). The plan consists of a loose grid; the buildings within each block are set parallel to each other, echoing the disposition of government buildings in the central sectors of Chandigarh. The early campus buildings by Chowdhury and the Gandhi Bhavan (1959–61) by Jeanneret sought to make buildings free-standing sculptures. The use of concrete as *the* building material and the concern for either orthogonal geometric or free-flowing forms established what has come to be known as Chandigarh architecture.

The Indian Institute of Technology [IIT] campus (1961–84) in New Delhi designed by Chowdhury and the Jawaharlal Nehru campus (1973+) by the CPWD and C.P. Kukreja (b.1938) follow the same architectural paradigm but show a much greater concern for buildings as space-makers than the Punjab University scheme does. If one is looking for precedents, the Delhi IIT campus has them in the courtyards of Oxbridge as well as in Le Corbusier's rationalism. The academic buildings consist of three-storey parallel blocks and a seven-storey block perpendicular to the longest of the three-storey blocks. The buildings are linked by covered walk-ways to form courtyards. The smooth concrete of the main blocks stands in contrast to the rough stone aggregate of the lecture theatres. The multi-storey staircases penetrating the courtyards add a Corbusian sculptural touch. Le Corbusier's influence was not always as strong or as clear.

Le Corbusier's architectural impact, like that of Gropius before him, was much stronger in north India than in the south. The Telecom Tower (1975) in Hyderabad is an example of a Le Corbusier-influenced building in the south but it was designed by a northerner, Jeet Lal Malhotra. It was not only architects directly associated with Le Corbusier who were influenced by his work: Doshi's design for the L.D. Institute of Indology (1952–62) in Ahmedabad might be expected but Charles Correa's later Sen House (1959–61) in Calcutta and Kanvinde's Balkrishna Harivallabhdas House (1964) in Ahmedabad owe just as substantial a debt to Le Corbusier. They were creative responses to the problems at hand using Le Corbusier's formal vocabulary.

The use of concrete and the horizontal banding in the L. D. Institute, the

The Indian Institute of Technology, Delhi

The L.D. Institute of Indology, Ahmedabad

parasol, a feature also used in a pergola for the Parekh House (Ahmedabad, 1967–8), by Charles Correa, and the *brise soleil* of Correa's design for the Cama Hotel (1958–9) in that city all reflect Le Corbusier's ideas. Indeed, the application of

The Sen House, Calcutta

a *brise-soleil* and similar concrete grids has become a hallmark of 'modern' façade design. Many commercial buildings have one to make them look modern if for no other reason.

On occasion it is Le Corbusier's specific geometric forms that captured the imagination of architects because they solved specific problems or coincided with specific Indian images. The vaulted roof is an example. In India its application has a long history in Buddhist Chaitya halls; its use by Le Corbusier in buildings such as the Masion Monal (1919), his weekend home (1935), and in later works, gave it an international cachet. Doshi used the form in the design of the Ahmedabad Textile Industries Research Association/Physical Research Laboratories housing (1960). He later raised it to a fine art in the design of his own office, Sangath (1979–80), the Chharodi Village Primary School (1979) and the Gandhi Labour Institute (1984) (Curtis, 1988; Bahga, Bahga and Bahga, 1993; Steele, 1998). Amongst other works in which the vault is used in a similar manner is the Times of India Office (1988) in Ahmedabad designed by Dhansukh Bhatt (b.1935).

Another example of Le Corbusier's influence is the deletion of spaces from a Platonic form to create a cubical object in space as in the Shodan House. A Platonic form has unbroken smooth surfaces. In these buildings the surfaces are broken not only by windows but by voids like terraces or simply open spaces. The Ramesh Patel House (1990) in Vadodara and the Jivan Jyot Estate (1997) in Surat by Anand M. Shirgaokar (b.1939) are instances of this method. The competition winning entry of Porius Master for the Headquarters of the Indian Institute of Architects Headquarters Building (1997) in Navi Mumbai is another example. In house design the type makes considerable climatic and cultural sense and both the houses by Shiraokar have received significant design awards.

Sangath, Ahmedabad

Ramesh Patel House,
Vadodara

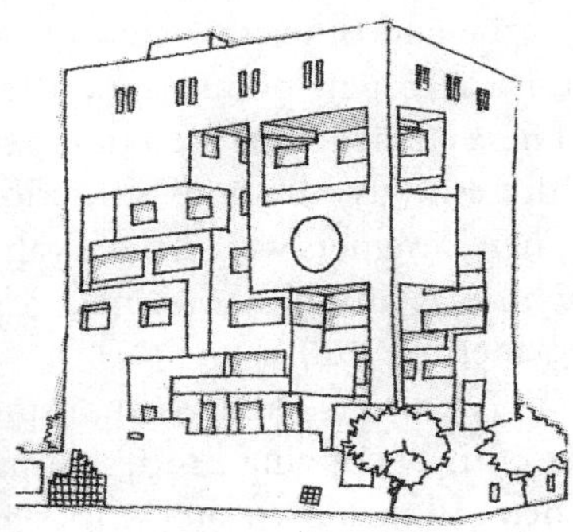

The proposed IIA Headquarters
Building, Navi Mumbai

Although a fairly standard structural type, the Sanskar Kendra (museum) in Ahmedabad is largely the model for the spate of concrete framed buildings with brick in-fill panels built across India. These buildings vary in type from houses to shopping centres to cinemas. The use of concrete in plastic forms had a significant impact throughout the world over the next two decades. A little more unusual is the way Le Corbusier's patterns were imitated by lay people for houses, water tanks and pump houses, in a Punjabi vernacular form.

In his own house (1959–60), Doshi demonstrated a stage in his long exploration of the forms, structure and spatial sequencing used by Le Corbusier, but within the Indian climatic and symbolic context. The overhanging roof, the interplay of light and shade, the jutting projections and the juxtaposition of brick and concrete all reflect the ideas of Le Corbusier. The method of handling breezes, the use of art works and the integration of built form and landscape, however, all relate the building to its tight site, close to other buildings, and its Ahmedabad context (Steele, 1998).

A number of other buildings completed during the 1960s and 1970s further illustrate Le Corbusier's influence. Sometimes this influence is obvious and at other times indirect even in the work of a single architect. The Akbar Hotel in New Delhi (1965–9), designed by Shiv Nath Prasad, draws heavily on the layout principles of Le Corbusier's Unité d'habitation (1947–52) in Marseilles (Le Corbusier, 1953). Prasad's design for the Shri Ram Centre (1966–9) is, in contrast, a more dramatic and innovative derivation from Le Corbusier's work. The Inter-State Bus Terminus (1969–71) in New Delhi designed by Rajinder Kumar (b.1936), and to a lesser extent, Doshi's designs for the Central Bank (1967) and Premabhai Hall (1975), both in Ahmedabad, are further examples of Le Corbusier's influence direct and indirect.

The Akbar Hotel is a thirteen-storey concrete slab building designed for the Delhi Municipal Committee. A service floor echoes the shopping floor of the Unité. It separates the common rooms below from the bedroom area above. Communal facilities, as in the Unité, are located on the roof but instead of being a creche and other services for a residential neighbourhood, they are the facilities for a transient population: a restaurant, a garden and a small outdoor theatre. These elements are used in the building for a sculptural effect against the skyline. Interestingly, the hotel's interiors were a mixture of the modern and the ethnic. Their designers were Laila Tyabji and Dale Keller, a Hong Kong-based American who was amongst the first to introduce Indian objects into modern interiors (Banerji, 1998).

Architects like Prasad, inspired by Le Corbusier, soon realised that they were essentially copying his design patterns rather than the design process that led to them. In their own later work they responded to this self-awareness. The Shri Ram Centre, which Prasad designed almost at the same time as the Akbar Hotel, was for a private trust that promotes dance, drama and theatre. It can be regarded as an example of the work resulting from the second phase of Le Corbusier's influence. In a true Rationalist manner Prasad explored the use of pure forms—the cylinder and rectangle—to create a piece of sculpture in reinforced concrete. The forms are by no means arbitrarily used: they express the different activities housed. The theatre is a cylindrical form and the rehearsal spaces are located in the rectangular mass. Other spaces are open-ended in character to meet the needs they serve.

Many architects who have worked for masters have taken a long time to evolve into their own people. They are confronted with the problem of paying homage to the master and yet having to develop their own identities without doing so in an arbitrary manner simply to be different. Many failed in this endeavour whether

The Akbar Hotel, New Delhi

The Shri Ram Centre, New Delhi

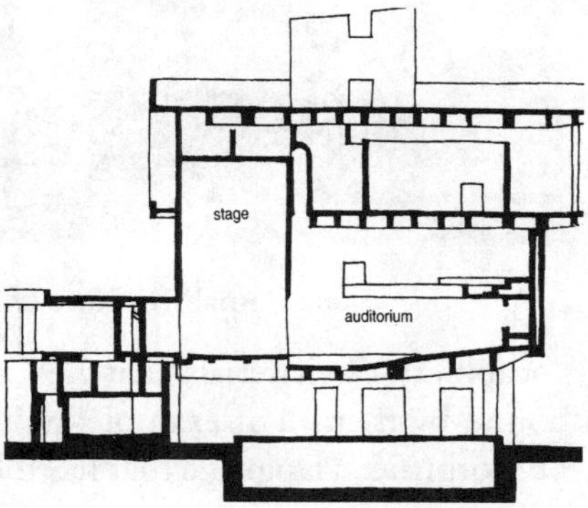

The Shri Ram Centre, cross-section

they worked for Le Corbusier in Paris, Frank Lloyd Wright at Taliesen, Kahn in Philadelphia or any other of the modern masters (Williamson, 1991). Doshi, of all Indian architects, was the closest to Le Corbusier. It took him some time to establish his own identity and, like many Indian architects on returning from their studies or work experience abroad, some time to deal head-on with India's own design concerns. His ability to abstract the essence of ideas from others and to use them wisely has earned him international recognition for his work.

Another architect who has gone through similar transformations, although younger and less well known internationally, is Satish Grover (b.1940). While his early work was strictly Modernist, inspired by Gropius and Le Corbusier, his designs for the Oberoi Hotel in Bhubaneswar (1983) and the Buddhist Temple in Pattaya, Thailand, are closer to the post-Modernist concepts of Robert Venturi (b.1925) in their intellectual aesthetic goals. Their forms are based on abstractions of traditional building patterns.

The fourth phase of Le Corbusier's impact on India can be represented by one of Grover's most recent works. In the Punjab State Institute of Public Administration Building (1996–7) in Chandigarh, Grover has blended Indian traditions with ideas drawn from Le Corbusier. Among the latter is the hierarchical organisation of components in terms of their importance. Thus the library and teaching spaces have precedence over the administration. Grover also uses the

The Punjab Institute of Public Administration, Chandigarh

vocabulary of materials that Le Corbusier used in Chandigarh. without being bound by them. For example, he uses curtain walls. It is additions like these to Le Corbusier's language that has the potential of enriching Indian architecture in the future.

The Architecture of Structural Dexterity

To a greater or lesser extent a central concern in architecture has always been with the enclosing of space and the methods whereby it is enclosed. There were many engineers and architects in India whose structural ideas, while contemporaneous with those of Le Corbusier, were independent of them. Indian architecture had a long engineering tradition dating back to the work of British military engineers in the nineteenth century and the indigenous buildings centuries earlier. In the twentieth century the analysis of structure was empirically based on scientific or quasi-scientific knowledge, but much of the application of this knowledge to architecture was Rationalist. The science enabled the exploration of a variety of ways of enclosing space whether or not such enclosures served well the supposed instrumental purpose of a building. These explorations have helped to build the science of structural analysis.

Collaborations between structural engineers and architects have yielded many innovative designs, and the structural explorations evident in the second generation of Modernist work in India were wide-ranging. Structural engineers popularised the architectural expression of forces of tension and compression in an artistic manner as exploited in Charles Correa's design for the Ahmedabad Cricket Stadium (1966) and Doshi's design for Ahmedabad's Tagore Memorial Hall (1971). The Hall is constructed of reinforced concrete folded plates 17 metres high and 15 centimetres thick. They span a distance of 33.5 metres. Mahendra Raj (b.1924) was the engineer on the latter design and his substantial range of collaborative works with architects include the Permanent Exhibition Complex (i.e., the Pragati Maidan, 1972) and the National Co-operative Development Corporation Building (1980) both in New Delhi, and the Salvacao Church (1974–7) in Mumbai (S. Prakash, 1986).

In the design of the Delhi Cloth Mills building, a post-tensioned box girder strung from hangar-like struts resting on arches was used by Morad Chowdhury (b.1933). A hybrid space-frame structure, it consists of staggered concrete walls, four columns on each side of the core and a box girder strung between columns. The box girder acts as a bridge between the lift core and the offices. There were other similar structural works. A space-frame structure of a poured-in-place octahedral lattice was used by Raj Rewal in the design of two major permanent exhibition halls in New Delhi: the Hall of Nations and the Hall of Industry (1970–4) (Bhatt and Scriver, 1990; Taylor, 1992). Engineering Consultants Ltd. assisted with both designs.

Architect-engineer collaborations also gave a number of buildings shell-roofs. A dramatic early example is the Venkateswara University Auditorium (1975) in Tirupati designed by S.L. Chitale and Sons. The roof is a 7.6 centimetre thick concrete surface, saddle shaped longitudinally and parabolic in cross section. The Salvacao Church designed by Charles Correa has simpler shell forms for its roofs while Pithavadian and Partners used a funicular shell roof in their design of the M.A. Chidambaram Cricket Stadium in Chennai. The roof of the stadium rests on wedge-shaped gutter beams that are supported on pairs of concrete columns. The columns also support the various layers of galleries.

Temporary buildings gave architects an opportunity to test ideas. In the Hindustan Lever Pavilion (1961) designed for an industrial fair, Charles Correa used random folded reinforced concrete plates gunited *in-situ*. The dramatic form encased ramps for circulation and platforms for exhibits (Correa, 1996). Such explorations, while hardly the norm, were by no means unique.

The Permanent Exhibition Complex, New Delhi

The Tagore Memorial Hall, Ahmedabad

The Venkateswara University Auditorium, Tirupati

The Salvacao Church, Mumbai

These architectural studies are important because many architects and architectural students had, by the end of the twentieth century, distanced themselves from the engineering aspects of building design and thus lost touch with what was historically a fundamental aspect of architecture. Many of the liveliest building forms have been inspired by structural possibilities. It is only when the display of structural dexterity is allowed to have a detrimental effect on the fundamental requirements of a design brief that problems for the users of buildings arise. Even in such circumstances a building may well be much admired by architects for its formal deviation from the norm! The danger is that in both cases—that is, caring about structural innovation too much and not caring about it enough—architects start to estrange themselves from society.

The Effect of Rationalist Thought

Many Indian architects of the era were inspired by the spirit of Independence and set out to explore all the possibilities for architecture that Rationalist thinking opened up. As such they were following Nehru in his effort to shape India to his own image of what the country should be. Modernist architectural thought paralleled Nehru's political ideology. By 1980, a substantial body of architectural work had been produced in India by a growing number of architects working within the Rationalist tradition. Their architecture, nevertheless, had an empirical content that grew from the 1950s onwards as they increasingly paid attention to the reality of contextual concerns.

Frank Lloyd Wright's image of the future city, his Broadacre City based on an agrarian model of democracy, was close to Gandhi's own philosophy. Like Gandhi's image of the future India, Wright's ideas had a small, but nevertheless significant, impact on India. Both presented possibilities that linger somewhere in many minds. The Rationalists' ideas, however, differed; they were fully in the foreground. Contemporary Rationalist architecture enriched the parallel development of work within the empiricist stream of thought and was enriched by it.

THE EMPIRICISTS

The second generation of Indian Modernists who followed Empiricist philosophies more closely than the Rationalist were influenced by a number of sources. The treatises and architecture of Frank Lloyd Wright and Louis Kahn were certainly important. The urban design ideas of these two international figures had, however, little impact on India. The Garden City philosophies reigned supreme and still do. In architecture within India itself, Joseph Allen Stein was beginning to build up a body of work that remains well known. It set a precedent for others to follow. In south India, Bennett Pithavadian's and S.L Chitale's offices were already providing examples that inspired others. Once Kahn's philosophies and designs became better known in India, they started to shape the thinking of a number of young architects more widely perhaps than the philosophies of other empiricists did.

The immediate result of Kahn's death in 1974 was that Raje took over the design of the IIM in Ahmedabad. Raje's design of a dining hall (1979) and the Management Development Centre (1982) are visually similar to Kahn's work and meld seamlessly with it. In a sense, Raje's work reflects the guru-student relationship traditional in India. Completed earlier, Doshi's design for the School of Architecture (1967–8) at CEPT also visually reflects Kahn's design vocabulary. Built of exposed brick and concrete, it is very different from his design for the L.D. Institute of Technology completed only five years earlier.

The School of Architecture derives its form from an educational as much as an aesthetic philosophy. The building consists of a semi-open basement-like

The Management Development Centre, IIM, Ahmedabad

The School of Architecture, CEPT, Ahmedabad

ground floor of classrooms linking raised hillocky lawns on one side with a sunken courtyard on the other. The first floor above is used for studios from where students and staff get views over the gardens on the north side while the south side has views over the courtyard and the playing area beyond. Being on an east-west axis, the spaces receive diffuse light from both north and south. An adjacent wing contains the library and administrative units. The design of the complex thus expresses the physical character of spatial divisions within a social environment. This building, in turn, shaped the thinking of younger architects. The design for the Navarang School (1974) by Anil Bakeri (b.1932) and Bipin Desai (b.1942) exemplifies the influence of Kahn's and Doshi's work on subsequent architecture (Chaudhry, 1989).

The patterns Kahn used in his India work have had an obvious effect but the use of his design principles by other architects has been subtle. The overall juxtaposition of buildings and the way they make spaces at the IIM in Ahmedabad is reflected in similar building complexes, for example, the Gujarat State Fertilizers Corporation Township (1964–9) in Vadodara designed by Doshi. The load bearing brick walls, arches and circular openings of Kahn's IIM building in Ahmedabad were picked up by Sachdev, Eggleston and Associates in the design of the Modern School (1974–8) in Vasant Vihar in South Delhi and by Mahendra Kothari (b.1942) in the Chinamaya Mission Centre (1975–9) in Ahmedabad. Over a decade later, Hiren Gandhi (b.1952) used similar forms in the design of the Municipal Market (1987) at Paldi in Ahmedabad (Chaudhry, 1989). Later still, Kahn's work was echoed in the Entrepreneurship Development Institute (1985–7) on the outskirts of Ahmedabad designed by Bimal Patel (b.1960).

The colourful distinction Kahn drew between master and servant spaces in

The Municipal Market, Paldi, Ahmedabad

the design of such buildings as the Richards Memorial Laboratories (1958–62) at the University of Pennsylvania is reflected in the Dudhsagar Dairy Complex (1971–4) designed by Achyut Kanvinde. Its reinforced concrete frames with brick in-fill panels and the tall ventilation ducts required to dissipate moisture in the making of powered milk echo ideas popularised by Kahn. They are also, more simply, sensible solutions to the problems at hand. Raje's design (in association with Kanvinde and Rai) for the Indian Statistical Institute (1970–6) in Delhi is another example of an architect drawing on Kahn's intellectual rather than

The Modern School, Vasant Vihar, Delhi

The Dudhsagar Dairy Complex, near Ahmedabad

geometric philosophy. By 1970, Raje's work had started to deal more expressly with local conditions than the immediate context of Kahn's IIM allowed.

The architecture in India within the Empiricist tradition drew on considerably more than Kahn's influence but his presence broadened it. For instance, the designs of Dhansukh Bhatt who completed his post-graduate studies at Yale with Paul Rudolph (1918–97) show the influence of that experience as well as the influence of Kahn (via Raje). His use of concrete and brick in the Central Institute for Plastic Engineering Technology [CIPET] building (1985) and in the earlier UCO Bank (1975–88), both in Ahmedabad, reflects the ideas of both architectural giants, Rudolph and Kahn.

With experience, second generation Empiricist work moved away from the direct influence of other architects to thinking more in terms of developing climatically and culturally appropriate four-dimensional design patterns to solve the problems at hand. Issues such as climate, heat and dust and winter chills, and social context became more and more important in designing briefs for buildings and in designing the buildings themselves. Often more important was simply the pragmatic job of getting a building erected quickly within a tight budget.

A REFLECTION

Le Corbusier brought into India a whole new vision of what architects and architecture could be, Kahn a view of how to handle materials and light, and the Eameses, a pedagogical philosophy. Without Le Corbusier would there have been the spate of 'Brutalist' concrete? Without Kahn, the forms and brickwork of his oeuvre? Their presence probably delayed Indian architects' move towards intellectual independence; it may have spurred a spurious search for artistic originality rather than solutions dealing with the world to be inhabited. Yet, with the wisdom of hindsight, one also senses that they brought an enhanced curiosity about the world with them—something that was lacking in the work of Gropius and his followers.

The innovative calibre of the architectural explorations exhibited in the second generation of Modernist work needs to be seen against the backdrop of the larger body of the more pragmatic work that was shaping the Indian scene. The hearts of India's major and minor cities alike were being rebuilt. Mumbai and New Delhi saw significant secondary developments taking place at nodal points within them and almost all the cities of the country started to see satellite towns being built around them—for instance, Navi Mumbai on the mainland opposite the Mumbai peninsula and Salt Lake City outside Calcutta.

In Mumbai, substantial development started to take place in the Nariman Point and Cuffe Parade areas and to the north in Cumballa Hill and Malabar Hill. In New Delhi, it was around Connaught Circus. South Delhi saw major developments such as Nehru Place. Anna Salai (still generally known as Mount Road) in

Chennai was much altered and in Calcutta there were new developments around the BBD Bagh area. Smaller cities also saw substantial building. Bangalore, in particular, was beginning to be transformed from a cantonment city into a Silicon Valley.

The Nariman Point area of Mumbai has become the city's new Central Business District. It contains a prestigious core area and a more crowded area of standard office buildings with somewhat differing façades. The former contains the Air India Building designed by John Burgee (b.1933) of Johnson/Burgee in New York, the Oberoi Towers and the Indian Express Building that I have already mentioned, the National Centre for the Performing Arts (1975–80, designed by Philip Johnson [b.1906], Burgee's partner). The prevalent architecture is, however, highly commercial—the 'Cash-on-Deliveri Towers' described by Salman Rushdie in his novel, *The Moor's Last Sigh* (1995).

The housing design of the period can be divided into two major types: the social housing of the PWDs and the plotted housing of individuals. There were, on a more limited scale, private apartment buildings. Designed by individual architects, they were beginning to show some innovations. In contrast, no significant new generation of social housing models was developed during the era. The first generation types continued to be built. The plotted houses, in contrast, were built in what has become known as the 'Modern Indian Vernacular'.

The Modern Indian Vernacular is the architecture of popular taste. It is certainly seen by its owner/clients as modern, up-to-date. Architectural intellectuals have little sympathy for it because of its seeming lack of cohesive ideas. (Bhatia, 1994a). It is an architecture of elements combined to have some meaning for the owners of buildings either because of their own associations or because they are being told by developers that it is meaningful. The middle class, like its Victorian ancestors, had acquired a status and like them, used a clutter of elements to display it.

There are substantial areas of Modern Indian Vernacular housing in all the major cities of India. These areas possess a unity of design through the very disparity of their individual components, each of which is clearly identifiable to its owners. Some of these buildings have been architect designed but others are the work of contractor-developers, the descendants of the mistris. The architectural work described in this book is the antithesis of the Modern Indian Vernacular although, as will be shown later, that vernacular has its place.

In the second generation of post-Independence Modernist buildings one sees the beginning of a shift away from a reliance on foreign architects and international architectural ideas to the home-born and bred. This statement does not seek to deny the continued influence of international ideas on Indian architecture, but it recognises that young Indian architects were beginning to place increasing reliance on Indian architects as role models. In addition, the work by Indian architects was beginning to receive international accolades—something necessary for the home-grown to be regarded as worthwhile at home. The result of this recognition was that architects outside India started querying what they were doing. The intensity of this self-examination should not be exaggerated but in India by 1980 the second generation of Modernist work had initiated the process of architectural reform. The next two decades took it much further.

5

Post-Nehru Modernist Architecture: 1965 to 1990

THE NEHRU era was one of unbridled optimism. His death in 1964 coincided with the beginning of a more pragmatic political period. Modernist architectural ideologies, especially those of the Rationalist stream, began to be challenged as their limitations became clear in the pragmatic world of professional practice. Many have declared the death of Modernist architectures, but they have evolved alive and well everywhere. They have been tempered by criticism but they still exist as expressions of modernism amongst important segments of the architectural community. However, no longer are claims made for the universality of Modernist design patterns. The limited model of the human being on which Modernist philosophies were based is widely recognised, if not whole-heartedly acknowledged. Much Modernist architecture and site planning has resulted not just in simple layouts, but boring ones (Venturi, 1966). Indian architects like Habib Rahman became fully aware of the limitations of the Modernist thought behind their own work. Rahman also recognised that the profession as a whole had learnt less than might have been expected from its experiences (M. Chatterjee, 1996). Yet the simple forms of Gropius, the lack of decorative features and the sculptural features and massive open spaces of Le Corbusier all have their place in architects' vocabularies.

In India, a number of forms of Modernist work continued to be built in the post-Nehru era. These forms overlapped considerably in nature and the distinctions amongst them are often blurred. Four streams of architecture are hesitantly identified here. One stream might be regarded as *pure Rationalist*, relatively unchanged in thought processes from that of the first two generations of such work in India. A second every-day version of it has been called *Utilitarian Modernist* as represented by much of the work of the Public Works Departments, Central and State-level, and the architecture of the commercial firms (Bhatt and Scriver,

The Civic Centre, New Delhi

1990). A third stream reflects the experiments with *architecture as sculpture* in which the shell of a building does not necessarily reflect the activities that it shelters but is in itself an expressive statement. A fourth is the work with a more empirical orientation that has, for want of a better term, been called *Neo-Modernist.* It represents what architects learnt from experiences with Rationalist designs in India. What emerged was a truly Indian Modernist architecture. A possible fifth stream is that influenced by the Brutalist buildings of contemporary British architecture. The work that might be classified as such was however really based on a whole different need—the need to recognise India's own architectural heritage.

While these developments were taking place, an important international architectural competition was held in India. It was for the design of a major complex of buildings—the Indira Gandhi National Centre for the Arts (1986)—to commemorate the life of Prime Minister Indira Gandhi (1917–84). It cannot stay unnoticed because it raised, indeed still raises, many questions about the appropriate architectures for India. A discussion of the competition is used to conclude this chapter and is a prelude to my analysis in the next chapter of the response to the limitations of Modernist architecture.

MODERNIST ARCHITECTURE

Many buildings in India have continued to be designed within the artistic paradigms established during the first two decades after Independence. Some of them have been designed by the same architects who executed the earlier work but there is other such work by a generation entirely new in terms of age, if not architectural ideology. Changes took place in Modernist design everywhere—for instance, it became more visually lively—but the work was carried on in the same intellectual vein as in the past.

Much of the Modernist work of the post-Nehru era consisted of commercial buildings. The more important of them stand out from their surroundings either because they are point blocks—towers—in areas of otherwise lower buildings or because they have design configurations that are a departure from the norm. Some do both. The point blocks include buildings such as the Vikas Minar (Tower of Progress, 1969), the headquarters of the Delhi Development Authority designed by Habib Rahman for the CPWD, the Reserve Bank of India building in Mumbai designed by Feroz Kudianwala, the Visvesvaraya Centre (LIC building, 1974–80) in Bangalore and the Kanchanjunga Apartments in Mumbai (1970–83) both designed by Charles Correa (the latter with Pravina Mehta), and the State Trading Corporation Building in New Delhi (1976–89) designed by Raj Rewal (b.1934). The second group comprises buildings such as the Life Insurance Corporation [LIC] Building (1986) in Connaught Place, also designed by Charles Correa, the National Cooperative Development Corporation building and the Delhi Civic Centre (1965–83), a tower block, the two last designed by Kuldip Singh (b.1934).

All three of these buildings are located in New Delhi. Buildings in other cities can be added to the list. The most prominent of them is the Madras Rubber Factory [MRF] administrative building in Chennai (1987–92) another work by Charles Correa, a building that owes a formal debt to his much earlier ECIL Office Building (1965–8) in Hyderabad.

The Delhi Civic Centre might be regarded as the exemplar of these buildings. It is a tapering eighteen storey structure, 28 metres wide at the top and 64 at its base. The form echoes those of the nearby Janta Mantar. It has a structural central core with four shear walls. The boldness of the handling of the off-the-shutter concrete is evidence of the lasting impact of Le Corbusier's work. The three storey high glazed entrance creates a strong emphasis on the façade facing the street. Four large bells salvaged from the clock tower of the old town hall hang in the monumental entrance hall (M. Chatterjee, 1985). A lawn sets the building back from the street so the structure is seen, in true Modernist style, as an object in space (although the cars, bicycles and people crowding the area Indianise the scene on weekdays).

The Visvesvaraya Centre is a concrete building with its sculptural quality confined within an orthogonal pattern. The LIC building in Delhi is different. It is a stone and mirror glass building under a steel framed parasol standing on a podium. The Kanchanjunga Apartments is one of the most photographed buildings in India. It consists of one and half storey split level three and four bedroom units. The building gets its visual distinction from its cellular form reflecting some of Correa's earlier housing explorations (see Correa, 1996).

The MRF building is a large horizontal structure with sweeping cantilevers and an internal atrium. It is located on a bend of Creams Road and its façade follows the street's curve. As such, unlike many Modernist buildings, it helps delineate the street. Its scale is also surprisingly compatible with its more traditional neighbours and comes from its horizontal massing. A major feature of the building is its curving, slatted pergola standing on massive pillars (also a feature in the ECIL complex in Hyderabad). On the ground floor are the common areas; each of the floors above is allotted to one of the company's major departments. The offices of the senior personnel are along the façade while the general staff are located in an open arrangement behind. The interior design is that of Mumbai-based Sudhir Diwan (Correa, 1996; Doctor, 1998). The whole scheme shows the continuity of development in Correa's ideas and how outside influences and his own thoughts are counterpoised in his work. Many of Correa's designs for example, show the precision of Scandinavian architecture that was much discussed in India, but do not appear to be directly related to it.

Leo Perreira (b.1943) is one Indian architect who had direct exposure to Scandinavian architecture through his studies at the Royal Academy for the Fine Arts in Denmark in the early 1970s. The meticulous design and detailing of his own house (1983) shows the influence. The house is traditional in layout with

The Visvesvaraya Centre, Bangalore

The Madras Rubber Factory Building, Chennai

The Perreria House, Ahmedabad, exterior

The Perreria House, Ahmedabad, interior

the dining room central and the other rooms linking off it. What sets the building apart are the long, low set openings, and the diverse floor and roof slab levels with the first floor recessed. The building achieves an integration of the Scandinavian spirit, the demands of India and Perreira's own architectural goals. The same observations can be made about two of his other works—the Church of Gaekwad-ni-Haveli (1979) and the Avanidhar Shah House (late 1980s). Their

The STC building, New Delhi

lines are pure and their geometries simple. In spirit they are allied with traditional Japanese thought.

The work of Japanese architects has had surprisingly little influence on India given the artistic links between India and Japan in Bengal earlier in the century. Japanese Metabolist architecture is, however, reflected in the work in this period of Raj Rewal, an architect educated in Delhi and London. He worked for five years in England and France before returning to India in 1962. The Metabolist attitudes towards design can best be seen in his design of the State Trading Corporation [STC] Building in New Delhi (1976–89), in his earlier Engineers India House (1978–83) and, perhaps, even in his design of the Permanent Exhibition Complex (1971–2). The STC Building has a large column-free framework with vertical shafts that allow various forms to be hung between them (Taylor, 1991, 1992). These building stand in emphatic contrast to Rewal's domestic architecture that has strong empiricist overtones.

There is a parallel body of work in India that is Modernist but to which the adjective 'individualistic' can hardly be ascribed. Known as Utilitarian Modernism, it provides the ground against which the more creative architectural works of the past half century provide the figures.

UTILITARIAN MODERN ARCHITECTURE

Many buildings continue to be designed in the modern equivalent of the PWD blueprint of the nineteenth century. They share with it a consistency in style across building types: housing, office buildings, district centres, schools, hotels and government administration buildings. It is an architecture that grew out of the commercial work of the large Anglo-Indian firms, particularly that of their Indian partners, as well as the engineering firms who were responsible for much building design. It is an architecture easy to caricature.

Utilitarian Modernist buildings have reinforced concrete structures and flat concrete roofs. Their façades have shading devices similar to a *brise-soleil*, simple projecting concrete slabs or more traditional chhajjas. The building shell does enable decorative elements to be added to the façade to give an identity to an organisation, or to tie a building to its locale. The spatial qualities of the interiors are seldom of concern. What is achieved is a neutral space of minimum ceiling heights that can be subdivided in many, many ways (Bhatt and Scriver, 1990). Often the buildings consist of a central core of lifts that services two wings. Architectural critics pay little attention to such buildings but given their number, the Utilitarian Modernist could easily be regarded as *the* architecture of contemporary India. It is a simple and simplified version of International Modernist architecture that has been adapted to Indian constructional conditions.

Some Utilitarian Modernist buildings have been extremely well crafted. As is often the case with a type, it is the earliest buildings that tend to be so. Yogakshema, the Life Insurance Company of India's building in Mumbai, designed by

The Life Insurance Corporation Headquarters, Mumbai

Gregson, Batley and King (GBK) in the early 1950s, might almost be regarded as an archetypal edifice of its kind. Like many subsequent government buildings it has a winged plan around a central entrance. In many such buildings the stairs are often vertically accentuated on the façade but not here. The building hugs and forms the curved street and the stuccoed façade is articulated to provide shading from the sun (Dwivedi and Mehrotra, 1995). It remains a good example of urban architecture.

Despite the variety of building types being designed in this manner, it is perhaps the housing schemes which best exemplify the work. HUDCO, DDA and the PWDs across India have produced large housing schemes with a remarkable consistency of appearance differentiated only by the socio-economic group for which they were built. With the increased hiring of consultants to do such housing, its nature has begun to evolve into a type that includes more elements of traditional forms—a Post-Modernist Utilitarianism (see Joglekar and Das, 1995).

While housing estates may be *the* exemplars of Utilitarian Modernism, much commercial architecture is similar. Nehru Place in South Delhi is a major Utilitarian Modernist complex and many of the 1980s buildings erected in Nariman Point in Mumbai are certainly of this nature. Nehru Place, a district centre, is a super-block island in which vehicular and pedestrian paths are segregated, enabling the creation of a raised internal plaza around which shops are located. The buildings stand on columns with the lower two floors that face the plaza recessed. Concrete columns, beams and slabs with infill panels structure the building. The buildings at Nariman Point are largely point towers but much the same description applies. Across the water along Cuffe Parade, the uniformity of buildings is even starker. Another body of contemporary work stands in strong contrast to them.

Low income housing, Chennai

Nehru Place, Delhi

ARCHITECTURE AS SCULPTURE

Some Modernist buildings combine what seem to be arbitrary external forms with the pragmatic interiors that are needed to serve the varied behavioural and aesthetic requirements of their users. The desire of architects was to exploit the technological capacities of materials, traditional and new, and the freedom of aesthetic expression they offer. It is not, however, a display of structural dexterity *per se.* Most of it has much greater symbolic intentions.

The sculptural quality of work in India parallels work elsewhere in the world even if much of it was built at a later date. The free form of Le Corbusier's chapel at Ronchamp (1950) had shown the way. The work in India is, however, much more closely related to, say the work of Jørn Utzon (b.1918) at the Sydney Opera House (1956–73) and Eero Saarinen (1910–60) in the designs of the Yale Hockey Rink (1955) and the TWA Terminal at Kennedy Airport in New York (1962). In engineering quality the Indian work owes much to the earlier structural engineering feats in the country.

Buildings of two spiritual sects—the Matrimandir (1970+) in Auroville designed by Roger Anger and the Baha'i House of Worship (1980–6) in Delhi designed by Fariburz Sahba, an Iranian architect based in Haifa—reflect international attitudes. The two are highly symbolic and relate to India not in their formal aesthetics but in the associational meanings of their geometric components. The meanings of the first are intellectual and have to be explained to be understood: they are not immediately obvious; those of the latter are more directly accessible. A third spiritual building, the Salvacao Church (1977), while highly sculptural, is less symbolic, reflecting more Correa's desire to create 'open to the sky' spaces (Correa, 1996).

The Matrimandir is an almost spherical temple. The main structure is part of a scheme that covers nine hectares and consists of the temple, an amphitheatre and gardens. The global form of the Matrimandir represents the egg of Vishnu. It is a huge chamber suspended on four pairs of piers. At the exact centre of the chamber is a crystal sphere onto which the sun's rays are directed by a heliostat. A processional path, whose beginning is defined by *chakras,* runs around the globe (Grandcolas, pen-name 'G', 1972).

The Baha'i House of Worship, a 1,300 seat auditorium, illustrates the simplicity of the Baha'i faith. The building sits on a podium and takes the form of the three ranks of nine petals of an opening lotus, a flower sacred to many people. The petals are made of reinforced concrete and are covered in white marble panels. The concrete, cement, silica sand and dolomite aggregate used in the building, like the marble cladding, is all white. The structure is organised to provide a series of skylights that filter light into the central hall. Surrounding the building are nine shallow reflecting pools over which air is drawn to cool the halls. The air is drawn up from the pools into the central hall from where a venturi effect draws warmed air out through a vent in the apex of the structure (Bahga, Bahga and Bahga, 1993).

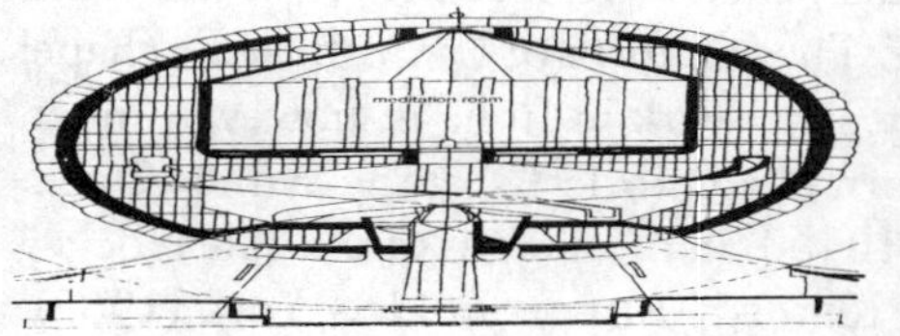

The Matrimandir, Auroville, cross-section

The Matrimandir, Auroville

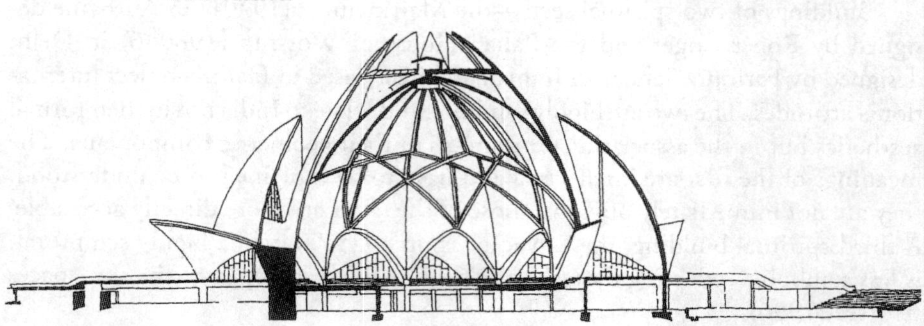

The Baha'i House of Worship, Delhi, section

The Baha'i House of Worship, Delhi

Designed for the Archdiocese of Mumbai, the Salvacao Church is a walled island of sculptural forms. It consists of a series of abstracted domical shell structures that create interlinked spaces. The shell roofs are ventilated at the top so that there is a continuous flow of air through the covered spaces although this system fails to cool the building on hot summer days. The church is Modernist in outlook and sculptural in the way that Le Corbusier's late work was, but its handling of space has a form not characteristic of much Modernist work. As such it represents a departure from pure Modernist design principles.

A secular building that shows the sculptural qualities of this line of Modernist architecture is the Belgian Chancellery and Ambassador's Residence (1980–3), designed by Satish Gujral (b.1945), a sculptor. Gujral's first architectural work was the Darayani House (1975), a renovation of a 1930s building. In it he played with level changes, bold staircases and visually linked spaces (Banerji, 1998). The

The Belgian Embassy, New Delhi

work for the Belgian Embassy is more dramatic. It is an expressionist statement in exposed brickwork. The ambassador's residence has been likened to a 'habitable ruin'. The overall impression that the complex gives is one of curvilinear forms, domes and arches, moulded together into a free flowing sculpture (Evenson, 1989; Tillotson, 1989; Gujral, 1993).

Many of the buildings in Auroville, both institutional and domestic, are highly personal sculptural statements. Educational buildings in the Cultural Zone of the settlement such as the Last School and the New Creation School, as well as national pavilions like the Bharat Nivas in the International Zone use a variety of materials to achieve the free-flowing plastic quality of organic forms. These forms are often borrowed from nature. The houses and workplaces in the Residential Zone are often images in sculptural form of the 'self' of their creators (see G, 1992).

The examples described here all fall within the Modernist ideal. Each building is a freestanding sculpture. The uniqueness of each reflects the perception of architecture as an individual artistic endeavour. The client is seen as a patron of the arts. It is a popular view amongst avant-garde architects but it is seldom as overtly achieved as in these examples.

NEO-MODERNIST ARCHITECTURE

Neo-Modernist architecture in India could well be regarded as the third generation of post-Independence modern architecture in the country. For Indian architects who were educated in the United States in the 1940s and 1950s it shows a third stage in their evolution, a maturation of their work into what could easily be called the Indian School of Modernist Architecture. For many younger Indian architects it is a product of their educations and the influence of contemporary work, not only of their Indian predecessors, but also of those around the world.

What occurred in India is that the ideas and thought behind Modernist architecture persisted but the forms associated with the architecture increasingly began to be adapted to local conditions. Some critics call this work the 'Second Modernism' because it represents an effort to create a regional architecture within the Modernist fold (Pallasmaa, 1988). The debt to the Modernist masters is fully acknowledged but their implicit approval, from beyond the pyre or grave, is not sought.

The precedents set by Gropius, Le Corbusier and Louis Kahn can be seen in much of this work, particularly that of Indian architects who worked closely with those masters. As these architects draw close to the end of their working lives one finds the influence of the masters being carried through them to those who have worked for them or been educated by them.

Representing the older generation are Indian masters, the old guard whose members are still astonishingly active both intellectually and professionally: Correa, Doshi, Kanvinde, Raje and many other important architects. If Kanvinde was Gropius' child, Doshi, Le Corbusier's and Raje, Kahn's, the three grand international masters can be said to have spawned many Indian grandchildren. With each succeeding generation the bloodlines become more heterogenous.

The Work of the Old Guard

The work of Achyut Kanvinde, Balkrishna Doshi and Anant Raje shows a rich intellectual growth and architectural maturation as each grew away from his mentor. Of the Indian masters, Charles Correa seems to have marched most to his own drum. The design efforts of this whole group also demonstrate a more widespread characteristic of Indian architects—the ability to adapt to varying conditions.

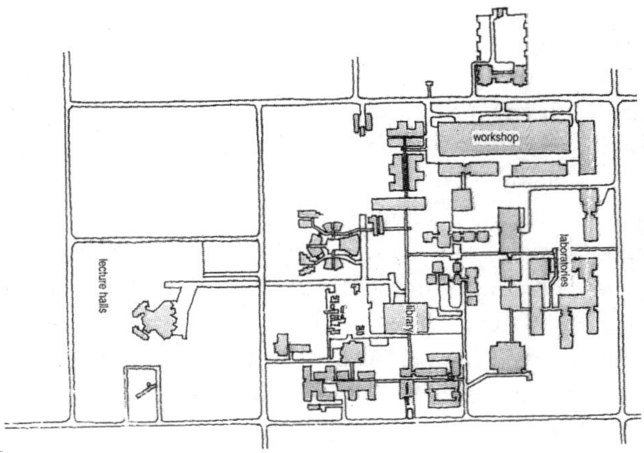

The IIT, Kanpur, plan

Kanvinde's design for the Indian Institute of Technology [IIT] at Kanpur (1959–66)

The IIT, Kanpur

differs significantly from his work at ATIRA in Ahmedabad less than a decade earlier. It is more spatially diverse, expresses its structural system more explicitly and also expresses the use of concrete in the way that Le Corbusier did at the Millowners' Association Building in Ahmedabad. The whole complex provides a much livelier environment than the Punjab University layout does.

Doshi's work of the 1980s in his own office, Sangath (1982), and the Gandhi Labour Institute (1984), both in Ahmedabad, illustrates the development of his work. These two buildings are dramatically different from say, the Institute of Indology, and, for that matter, from the 1977+ design of the Indian Institute of Management in Bangalore which has neo-Vernacular overtones. Both Sangath and the Gandhi Labour Institute employ vaults that Doshi and Raje had used much earlier in their careers in the design of low-cost housing. Sangath is set in a walled compound on a podium that descends in a series of terraces to a landscaped garden. A long barrel vault roofs the studio while two shorter ones cover the guestrooms and small work stations. They are fabricated of cylindrical tiles sandwiched between thin ferro-cement shells and covered with white ceramic shards. The Gandhi Labour Institute is a three-part complex consisting of academic, residential and dining blocks that enclose a courtyard. Like Sangath, the Institute is an island set in a walled compound. (M. Chatterjee, 1985; Bhatt and Scriver, 1990; Bahga, Bahga and Bahga, 1993; Steele, 1998).

Few Indian architects have maintained as steady an intellectual and formal architectural mood as Raje. He continues to design new components at the Indian Institute of Management in Ahmedabad. In doing so, he has maintained Kahn's themes. His work of the 1970s in other buildings, such as the Indian Statistical Institute (1970; with Kanvinde, Rai and Chowdhury) in Delhi and the Semi-Wholesale market in Navi Mumbai (1974-8) follow the same idiom. However, his effort to create a regional architecture is clearer in his work for a number of public agencies during the 1980s and 1990s. These buildings include the Galbabhai Farmer's Training Institute (1981) and the Indian Institute for Forest Management (1988), both near Bhopal, and the Headquarters of the Bhopal Development Authority (1991). In these buildings he strove to create a unity and a 'gentle urbanism' using screens and arcades.

The geometry of the Indian Institute of Forest Management shows Raje's high regard for the work of Louis Kahn in its use of arched forms and concomitant patterns of solid and void and light and darkness. At the same time, the complex shows the emergence of other influences in Raje's contemporary work. They include the spatial organisation schema of the palaces of the Deccan. Despite such glances at the past, the overall design of the Institute remains strictly Modernist. The plan is based on the segregation of uses; the structural order follows (Bahga, Bahga and Bahga, 1993). If anything, the design of the building parallels recent deconstructionist thought processes in the layering of orders. The basic order is rigid, but the superimposed orders are based on more haphazard geometries.

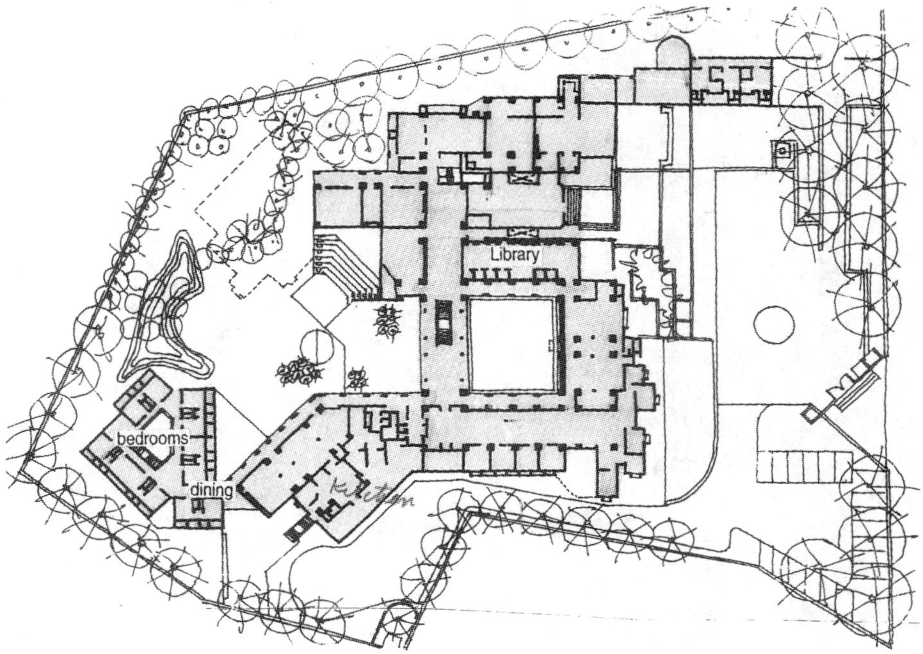

The Gandhi Labour Institute, Ahmedabad, plan

The Gandhi Labour Institute, Ahmedabad

Correa sought, and continues to seek, an architecture of 'open to the sky' spaces based on his earlier housing explorations and the disaggregating of cellular living spaces. His Kanchanjunga Apartments could be included here; but perhaps

The Headquarters of the Bhopal Development Authority

a building already mentioned, the Salvacao Church (1977), is a better example of what is meant here by Indian Modernist work as opposed to Modernist work in India!

The Work of the 'Next' Generation

The next generation is identified as much by the sequence of work within a particular genre as by the age of the architects involved or even who they were. The architecture was generally in the same idiom as that of earlier designs but noticeably different visually. A more radical departure did occur in the 1980s when some architects, old and young, turned to new referents in search of a new architecture. These referents included the work of architects other than the modern masters, literary criticism and post-structuralist thinking, postmodernist thought. This work will be considered in the next chapter. Here the concern is with the architects whose work, or at least some of it, continued in the basic Modernist fold. Many of their most notable designs were of institutional buildings—a major building type of the era.

One of the difficulties in designing institutional buildings is to provide their users with a feeling of psychological warmth and intimacy while meeting the institution's primary goals. A number of buildings of the era succeeded in doing so using very different mechanisms. Sen Kapadia's design for the Sainik Guesthouse (1982) for retired military personnel and the Institute for Food Science (1985), both in Bhopal, demonstrate his search for a simplicity in the line and form of buildings while maintaining some level of intimacy. The Sainik Guesthouse consists of commercial space on the ground floor with dormitories above. On the top floor are private guestrooms. The circulation space is functional in Modernist terms to allow for the ease of movement. The vertical circulation is centrally located so that guests can move easily to the wings on either side. The building is particularly interesting in the way it handles sunlight. Skylight shafts abut the core and jut into the skyline. The third, fourth and fifth floors are recessed with each layer being angled slightly to enable the south side to be overshadowed by the layers above. The result is that there are some restrictions in the ease of movement—something strict Modernists would decry (Bhatt and Scriver, 1990).

Another very different institutional building seeking to be other than institutional is the Centre for Environmental Education (CEE, 1988–90) in Ahmedabad, designed by Neelkanth Chhaya (b.1951) and Kallol Joshi (b.1951). It is a face-brick complex of educational facilities and offices that has a considerably greater warmth than many institutional buildings. It also demonstrates a concern for the sequential experience of spaces, of the opening and closing of vistas as one moves through a complex. At the CEE this is helped along by the topography and planting.

The same concern for sequential experience is also exhibited in building complexes such as the Visitors' Hostel (1990) at the Jawaharlal Nehru Centre for Advanced Scientific Research [Nehru Science Centre] of the Indian Institute of Science campus in Bangalore. Designed by Sanjay Mohe (b.1955) of the local firm of Chandavarkar and Thacker, the Visitors' Hostel has strong Indian antecedents in the intracacies of mohallas and pols in its physical form. The social cohesion of a hostel makes the concept successful. The breaking down of the scale to domestic levels is also reflected in the aesthetic order (Chandavarkar, 1989).

A notable proportion of the architectural work of the last three decades of the twentieth century has focused on the play of solids and voids and the intertwining of geometric patterns. The Visitors' Hostel at the Science Centre is by no means unique in that respect. The Indian Tourism Development Corporation's Ashok Hotel, Agra (1982), designed by Arvind Gupta and Associates, the earlier Hotel Mughal Sheraton, Agra (1974–7), the work of the ARCOP Design Group, the later Babylon Apartments in Calcutta (1983–7) designed by Dulal Mukerjee, and the K. L. Institute for Deaf and Mute Children (1975–7) in Bhavnagar, designed by Dhansukh Bhatt, all illustrate the evolution of Modernist geometries into richer and more interest-holding forms.

The Centre for Environmental Education, Ahmedabad

The Visitors' Hostel, Nehru Science Centre, Bangalore

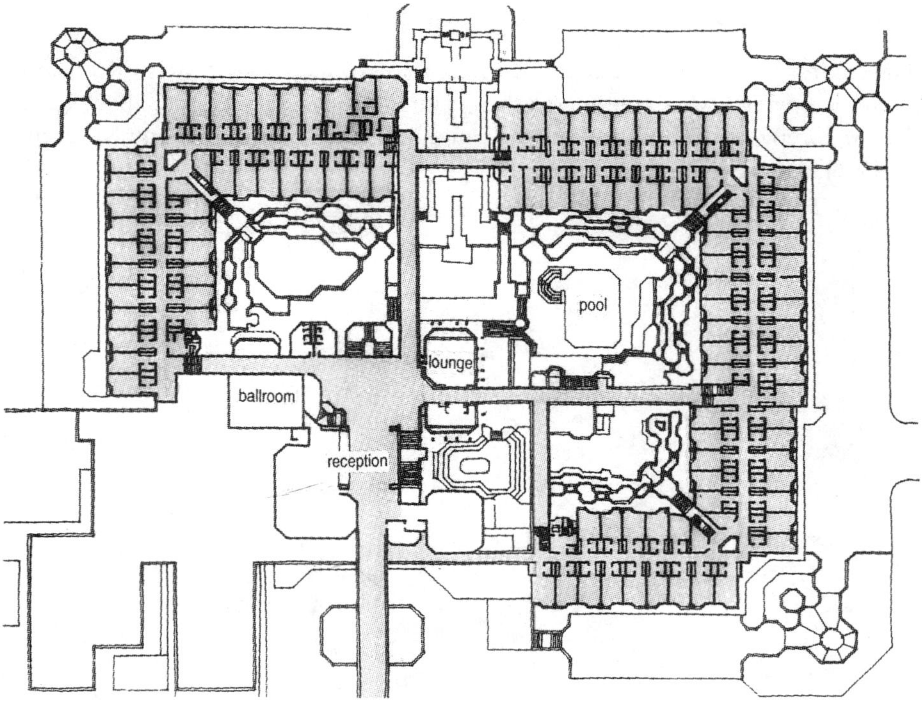

The Mughal Sheraton Hotel, Agra, plan

The Mughal Sheraton Hotel, Agra

The Sheraton, an Aga Khan award winner in 1980, is a low-rise brick structure surrounding a series of garden courts. Incorporated in the building are patterns from Mughal architecture that provide reference points to the nearby Taj Mahal and Fatehpur Sikri (M. Chatterjee, 1985). This kind of inclusion of vernacular elements, but on a larger scale intellectually and physically, is a hallmark of post-Modernist work and so will be considered more fully in the next chapter.

A similar play with solids and voids occurs in The Babylon Apartments. Built on a narrow block, the building consists of a variety of setbacks and projections bas-ed on a module of 27 squares. Each apartment has a terrace and the building is much covered with vines and other plants (Bahga, Bahga and Bahga, 1993). It is this type of variety that sets the building apart from the strictly Modernist work of the earlier generation.

The Babylon Apartments, Calcutta

Bhatt, who has been called a 'disciplined minimalist', gave the school for deaf and mute children a strong periphery of buildings and a heavily treed central court dominated by an aviary. The classrooms are single storeyed strung together by a meandering yet geometrically simple corridor. The roof of the classrooms is a 75cms thick reinforced brick masonry slab that keeps the ambient temperature at a comfortable level on even the hottest days. Each classroom has a skylight so placed that the teacher's face is illuminated and his or her lips can be clearly seen. The administrative and dining block are larger but the scheme combines to form a unified whole. The objective was to provide an environment at a scale in which children feel comfortable (Pandya, 1993). A number of Indian Modernist buildings have been at the other end of the physical scale in size.

The SCOPE (Standing Conference of Public Enterprises) Building (1980–9) is an almost 100,000 square metres quasi-megastructure in which Raj Rewal explored the integration of bold massing and structural ingenuity. Its square modular system and corner towers make it look like a citadel. The ten-storey building, daily home to seven thousand employees, is a city within a city. As Modernist site planning preferred, the building, large as it is, sits as an object in space. It is also Modernist in the way its structure is expressed and the manner

The K.L. Institute for Deaf and Mute Children, Bhavnagar

in which its service and air-conditioning ducts extend above the roofline like chimneys (Taylor, 1991, 1992). In other words, these elements are clearly visible to the passer-by.

While churches in India are frequently designed with some form of Modernist expression, there are fewer such Hindu or Sikh temples amd mosques. Amongst many others, St Matthew's Church (early 1990s) by Ram Dadoma and Associates,

The SCOPE Building, New Delhi

St Mary's Cathedral, Varanasi (1990–3) designed by A.G. Krishna Menon, and the Church of God (Full Gospel) of the same era in Chandigarh are Modernist examples. The Ati Rudra Yagnasthala (1983) near Hardwar is traditional in plan only. Achyut Kanvinde had a free hand with its appearance. Similarly, the Gayatri Shaktipith (1983), located in Billimora, Gujarat, designed by the Design Workshop, has a plan that retains the traditional *yagna mandap,* high plinth, *sabha mandap, garbha griha* and *pradakshina* path. The concern for the symbolic use of light and the series of cowl-shaped alcoves and main domes give the building an overall plastic quality. Whether the temple's resemblance to a church is conscious or not is unclear; but it is in much the same manner that seventeenth and eighteenth century Hindu temples in Goa have forms similar to Baroque churches (Pereira, 1995).

At the younger end of Indian Modernists are architects such as Bimal Patel (b.1960). It is not surprising that his work continues, but develops, the ideas of

St Mary's Cathedral, Varanasi

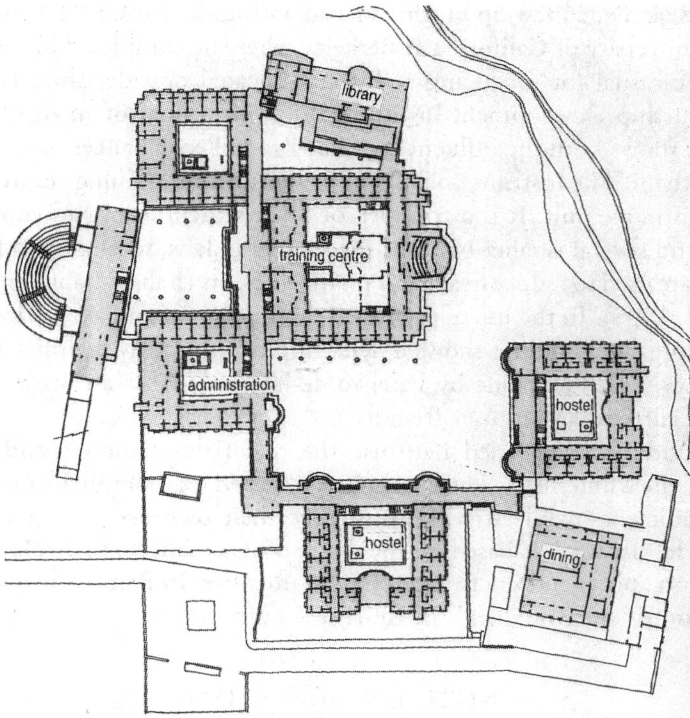

The Entrepreneurship Development Institute, Ahmedabad, plan

The Entrepreneurship Development Institute, Ahmedabad

Kahn and Raje. Patel grew up in Ahmedabad and studied at CEPT before going on to the University of California at Berkeley where he completed his doctorate, something unusual for practicing architects. Located outside Ahmedabad, the Entrepreneurship Development Institute (1985–7), winner of an Aga Khan design award, shows both the influences of Patel's intellectual ancestors and deviations from them. The Institute consists of an auditorium, training centre, library, and administrative unit. It is a complex of brick structures organised around a courtyard and several smaller outdoor spaces. Verandahs, recessed windows and thick walls are used to reduce heat loads on the interiors (Bahga, Bahga and Bahga, 1993; Patel, 1999). In the use of the raised plinth, the rich use of brickwork and in its detailing, the building shows a departure from strict Modernist attitudes. It also shows the effort made by Patel to de-institutionalise an institution—to make it, in current jargon, user-friendly.

The buildings mentioned here use the materials—concrete and brick—favoured by the Modernists. Their architects searched for a simplicity of form and structural efficiency while striving to achieve their own aesthetic goals. Some Indian Modernist work is based on the desire of its architects to display a building's structure, pipes and ducts in an 'honest' manner. In Britain the work went under the rubric of 'Brutalism'. In India it should not.

A NOTE ON BRUTALISM

A number of young European, particularly British, architects from the 1950s down to the 1970s sought a bold intellectual clarity in their work in an attempt to divert critical attention from what they perceived to be the architectural 'establishment'. The Brutalists reacted negatively, indeed with hostility, to the 'New Humanism' and the 'New Empiricism' that characterised the general response to the perceived limitations of Rationalist theory. The mainstream response was to look more keenly at the realities of life. The Brutalists would have nothing to do with this approach. While the term *Brutalism* mocked what its proponents saw as the compromising of Modernist attitudes, it also had its own artistic agenda.

The Brutalists admired the puritanism of classical architecture and they abhorred the concealment of materials and construction techniques. Construction methods had to be expressed; pipes and ducts had to be celebrated. These elements were thus exposed to view and painted in bright colours. Such expressions were regarded as 'honest'. In India, the reasons for its use were different from the need for 'honesty'. Indeed the use of Brutalist concepts in Europe probably simply paralleled what was happening in India.

In the vernacular buildings of India materials such as mud-brick and stone have always been used in a rough manner. Architects, particularly in northern India, in looking at the finishes of the *beton brut* of Le Corbusier must have been reminded of the villages and towns of Rajasthan that they so admired. Many

Indian buildings of the 1970s, in particular, seem to reflect Brutalist ideas. Vikram Bhatt and Peter Scriver (1990) suggest that it was the ethic—the need to be frugal—rather than the aesthetic of Brutalism that guided Indian work. Whatever the intellectual basis, the contemporary work of Achyut Kanvinde and of the three architects of the Design Group (Morad Chowdhury, Ranjit Sabikhi and Ajoy Chowdhury) amongst many others such as Raj Rewal and Kuldip Singh, could be analysed in Brutalist terms. All their work, as is argued in the next chapter, owes a greater debt to vernacular architecture and to the search for an Indianness than to Brutalism *per se.*

THE IGNCA COMPETITION

Almost a side event in the development of modern architecture in India, but important because of the questions it raised, was the competition for the Indira Gandhi National Centre for the Arts [IGNCA] held in 1986. The 10.2-hectare site for the Centre lies on the northern side of the Mall in Delhi where it intersects Janpath and opposite the National Archives building designed by Luytens. The competition brief listed a vast array of facilities for the study and display of India's fine and performing arts heritage. Above all, perhaps, was the goal of gaining an internationally recognised symbol of modern India in the way that Chandigarh had done earlier. The competition drew almost two hundred entries from forty-six different countries. The jurors included such architectural luminaries as Doshi, Kanvinde, Fumihiko Maki (b.1928) and James Stirling (1926–92) (Huet, 1987; R. Grover, 1991)

The location of the site within the bold imperial scheme of Lutyens and Baker, the desire to commemorate the life of Indira Gandhi and to boost the image of Indian culture raised many questions about the direction in which Indian architecture should go. Ralph Lerner (b.1949), an educator at Princeton University with a practice in that city, designed the winning entry. A scheme by Gautam Bhatia was placed second. Significant Indian entries also came from such well-known architects as Raj Rewal, Romi Khosla, Chandra Prakash Kukreja and Anil Laul.

The winning scheme, unanimously chosen by the jurors, recognised the importance of the existing context and sought a monumentality in design. It is a neo-classical, courtyard composition that integrates its parts into a whole. Certain components of the scheme (e.g., the Sutradhara, the administrative building of the complex) stand out as figures against the ground of other buildings. Visually, the elements of the scheme reflect certain Indian building types, such as the temple shikhara and parts of Fathepur Sikri, but questions (probably impossible to answer) about its capturing an Indian spirit have been widely raised. Lerner revised the scheme in 1989 but its essence remains unchanged.

The Bhatia entry sought to evoke the symbols of a city, like Delhi, by a river.

If Lerner's scheme was neo-classical, Bhatia's was strictly Modernist. What the competition, and the responses to the entries, showed is that by the mid-1980s, Indian architects were having to come to grips with a wide variety of past histories and aspirations for the future. Certainly the quest for an Indian identity was uppermost in many Indian minds.

Construction on the IGNCA progresses. Lerner continues as project director with the basic design work being carried out in Princeton while much of the interior work and supervision continues under the direction of Jasbir Sawhney, an experienced Delhi architect chosen by Lerner as a collaborator. The first buildings are now under construction. One significant change in the overall design is that the east west passages that link the spaces are now to be enclosed and air-conditioned. One Indian tradition gives way, perhaps unnecessarily, to the desire for greater comfort! Lerner was not, however, comfortable with that decision, which was made by others (Lerner, 2000).

A REFLECTION

What unifies the otherwise diverse set of buildings mentioned in this chapter is the purity of their central ideas and the paucity of any added decoration. They show no desire to follow the intellectual basis of contemporary post-modern work in Europe or America in which traditional forms were abstracted to give a sense of locale to buildings; neither do they follow the more superficial post-modernism of flamboyant forms of architecture displayed both in India and abroad. They also show little inclination to use vernacular elements literally. What the architecture does do is adapt narrow Modernist ideas to the necessities of India. Contrary to Habib Rahman's observation that little was being learnt from experience, the criticism of Modernist architectural philosophies *was* slowly penetrating the professional world.

The Modernist architecture of the post-Nehru era had attempted to build on earlier work. One started to see a visually richer set of building patterns than the Bauhaus desire for purity would allow. There was also the recognition that merely saying one is designing for climatic and cultural conditions is not enough. An architect should really do so. In the work described in this chapter, not only building patterns but also siting patterns remained Modernist. Little attention was paid to how buildings might be designed to enhance their contexts. This failure was one of the universal problems of both Rationalist and Empiricist lines of thought. There was a partial adaptation to India at the level of the design of individual buildings, but buildings continued to be thought of as objects in space and not as environment-making elements. At heart, much Modernist architecture was anti-urban. James Stirling, the British architect whose own Modernist credentials cannot be challenged, noted that 'Ninety percent of Modern Architecture [is] boring, and barren and disruptive when placed in older cities'. During the 1980s

Philip Johnson added: 'There is no doubt that our cities are uglier than they were fifty years ago'. The Modernist work described in this chapter attempted to respond to such observations. At the same time, Modernist architectural thinking was being challenged more radically by post-modern ideology. Some Indian architects remained indifferent to that challenge; yet others took it up.

The Indian Institute of Management, Bangalore

6

Post-Modernist Architecture: 1975 to 1995

THE TERM 'post-modern', now used in literary analysis as well as the social sciences, semiology and philosophy, implies an increasing fragmentation in life—a breaking apart of monolithic structures (Ghirado, 1996). Post-modernism has had a profound effect on architecture.

In architecture, Post-Modern, as a proper noun, seems to reflect three tendencies. They are: (1) the use in design of past elements of form in an abstract manner; (2) a drawing on the vernacular past to indigenise architecture, and (3) a recognition of the variety of problems that exist in a society and attempts to address them directly. Purists accept only the first to be truly Post-Modernist architecture but the other approaches are also part of the post-modernist world. Indeed, in India they are the more important. Out of the second emerged an architecture that can rightly be called *the* Modern Indian Architecture if one insists on there being one. Out of the third came a variety of approaches to dealing with the concerns that, if not unique to India, are certainly present in the country.

A number of other advocacies came to the fore as a response to Modernist architecture and to much of the everyday commercial architecture of the country. Akin to those architects rediscovering the utility of looking at vernacular architecture were those seeking a direction in the Shilpaic canons. It is a direction gathering adherents. The black sheep in the architectural family has been the Modern Indian Vernacular—the highly eclectic architecture of much of the middle class—introduced in the previous chapter. Not directly related to any of these efforts is the Community Architecture Movement. Its goal has been to bring architectural knowledge and skills to bear on improving the lives of people living in slums.

In looking at these implicit critiques of the earlier work of the profession one draws the conclusion that different problems require very different solutions. The

Post-Modernist explorations of the 1970s and 1980s that paralleled in time the work described in the previous chapter set the scene for what evolved in the last five years of the twentieth century.

POST-MODERNIST ABSTRACTIONISM

If one accepts Post-Modernist architecture as only that involving the application of abstracted traditional building design motifs and patterns in new architecture, in India, this kind of work began independently. The goal was to make buildings meaningful to lay people. Other efforts have been made to achieve this end but they have taken design elements from the past literally as in the earlier Indo-Saracenic work of British architects and that advocated by the Modern Indian Architectural Movement during the 1930s and 1940s. In those works little effort was made to transform historic shapes into abstract representations of them. The difficulty Post-Modernist architects have had is in making the abstractions recognisable to others.

A well-known modern Indian architect used abstract forms from the past to convey a continuity in meaning long before the international Post-Modernist

The Mazar of Fakhruddin Ali Ahmed, New Delhi

debate and Venturi's book, *Complexity and Contradiction in Modern Architecture* (1966). In the Mazar of Maulana Azad (1960), the Rabindra Bhavan (1961) and the Mazar of President Fakhruddin Ali Ahmed (1975), Habib Rahman used abstract variations of historic precedents. In the first of these projects he used an abstraction of the Islamic arch, in the second, an abstraction of chhajjas and jaalis and in the third, an abstraction of the silhouette of the Taj Mahal.

The outstanding recent work of this type in India is that of Romi Khosla (b.1941) who heads GRUPINDIA. The School for Spastic Children (1985–95) in New Delhi is an example of his work of the time. It clearly owes an intellectual debt to Venturi (Editors, *Mimar*, 1989). The school exhibits Khosla's use of 'exaggerated iconic forms' and his belief that a building should reflect a psychological concept so there is also a 'narrative' to it. His idea was to create a protective womb almost as an abstraction of the rock-cut cave temples at places such as Ajanta (Bhatt and Scriver, 1990). The building does indeed provide a sheltered environment with a courtyard open to the sky. To ease movement for the pupils, ramps and wide openings have been provided and there are no high plinths. Tall and deep recesses evenly spaced along the façade run from ground to roof. They include balconies that alternate in shape—squares and semi-circles. The forms of the tiers of windows with their sloped profiles are echoed in the low outer wall. This building may be the outstanding example of its Post-Modernist type but there are others of note.

Contemporaneous work included the Madani Hall and Mahmoodia Library (1986) located adjacent to the Masjid Abdul Nabi in Delhi. Designed by M.A.U.

The School for Spastic Children, Delhi

The Madani Hall and Mahmoodia Library, Delhi

Khan (b.1931) and M. Elahi (1933–2000) of Asema Architects, the layout of the four-storey building, consisting of an entrance hall, museum, seminar room, hall, research library and terrace, is standard but its external appearance is not. The building's domical Islamic arch forms and stone work is a simplified version of a historic wall type. To European critics it is probably not abstracted enough to be regarded as true Post-Modernist work but it succeeds in being readily understandable to lay-people—the original goal of Post-Modernists.

In the Oberoi Hotel (1983) in Bhubaneswar, the way that past models have been abstracted differs radically from the examples above. The hotel was designed by Satish Grover who abstracted, in plan form, the linear movement pattern from the *mandapa* to the *garbha griha* that structures the Hindu temple. In the hotel, the sequence culminates in a large courtyard facing the guestrooms; a Buddhist *vihara* is the precedent. The logic is highly intellectual. The casual visitor is only aware that there is a clear and interesting sequencing of spaces. It is possible that the sequence subconsciously resonates with visitors because of their own religious experiences. If so, it achieves its purpose.

A number of religious buildings might well be regarded as Post-Modernist in the terms considered here. The Buddhist Temple (1987) in Pattaya, Thailand, like Bhubaneswar's Oberoi Hotel, was designed by Satish Grover. It 'assembles the elements of Buddhist architecture as the mind reconstructs images from memory' (J. Shah, 1992). The *chaitya* hall, *torana* and *stambha* are reduced to simpler geometric forms that signify them' (J. Shah 1992). The Prarthana Mandir (1972) of the Ramakrishna Mission Vidyapith in Purulia, West Bengal, designed by Sunil Pal and Ramananda Bandopadhyay is an austere structure of interlocking stone wall masses. A mushroom-like dome caps a low tower instead of the traditional *shikhara*. It is decorated with abstracted leaf forms symbolising the *panchavati*.

The Dakshin Delhi Kalibari Temple (1983+) designed by Sumit Ghosh (b.1942) and Suchitra Ghosh (b.1945) might also be regarded as a Post-Modern temple. The innovative design parallels significant changes in the liturgy of the Bengali sect. The *garbha griha*, for instance, has been thrown open to the worshipper and its amalgamation with the *sabha mandapa* creates a temple within a temple. Nevertheless, traditional liturgical symbols retain their importance. So too in the architecture. The *garbha griha* has an abstracted traditional 'Bengal roof'. The superstructure of the temple has a conoid representing the traditional *kalibaris* and the *shikhara* becomes a small crown (Menon, 1990). Still incomplete, the roof will have a copper *kalasha* over it.

This body of work, in theory if not appearance, represents a major intellectual endeavour to respond to the limitations of Modernist architectural ideology. It is in particular a response to the Rationalist branch of Modernist thought and its belief that the symbolic meaning of buildings results from responses, whether intellectually or biologically based, to the purity of line and the inter-play of basic iconic forms. The architecture described here is no mere copying of the past but

Dakshin Delhi Kalibari Temple, Delhi

a creative response to what was perceived to be an aesthetic lacuna in Indian architecture. The 'Neo-Traditional' architecture has been, perhaps, more successful in filling it.

THE NEO-TRADITIONAL: *THE* MODERN INDIAN ARCHITECTURE?

At the end of the 1960s, a number of events coincided suggesting to Indian architects that looking at one's own heritage within one's own cultural frame might be the way forward. One was the world-wide recognition that Modernist architecture, both in township layouts and in buildings, had failed to achieve the very goals it had set itself in manifestoes such as the Athens Charter (see Sert and CIAM, 1944). In particular, it became obvious that while certain building patterns might be appropriate universally at a generic level they had to be substantially adapted to local conditions to meet their goals. Another development was the emergence of environment-behaviour studies as a core contributor to architectural educational curricula (Rapoport, 1977; Lang, 1987). They challenged the narrowness of the Modernists' definition of function. Perhaps the most important event of all was the celebration, in 1969, of the centenary of Mahatma Gandhi's birth: as a result his ideas were revisited. Inevitably, questions were raised about the directions in which architecture was headed.

The 1964 Architecture without Architects exhibition organised at New York's Museum of Modern Art by Bernard Rudofsky and the accompanying book (Rudofsky, 1964) and Hasan Fathy's work in Egypt (Fathy, 1969) gave the study of vernacular architecture a boost. Since 1970 many architects have been looking at how patterns of traditional houses fitted Indian ways of life and, architectonically, how they also create patterns of light and shade, interior volumes and exterior masses. In India, the importance of looking at oneself and one's own traditions was emphasised by a number of leading architects. Amongst them were such strong Modernists as Achyut Kanvinde, Charles Correa, B.V. Doshi and Ranjit Sabhiki. Less renowned voices belonged to Ashish Ganju, Kulbushan Jain, Minakshi Jain, Uttam Jain, Rewati Kamath, Vasant Kamath and Jai Sen. 'It was as if the ghost of Claude Batley had returned to haunt a few architects' (Malay Chatterjee, 1985). One cannot really talk of any concerted Neo-Traditional architectural movement. There was no united effort comparable to that of CIAM [Congrès Internationaux d'Architecture Moderne] nor the Modern Indian Architectural Movement of Sris Chandra Chatterjee. It just so happened that many architects sought inspiration from vernacular traditions. What emerged could easily be called the truly 'Modern Indian Architecture'. It paralleled the attempt, internationally, to develop or maintain a unique architectural identity in the face of universalising trends.

There have been two clear lines of thought about how the past can best serve present needs. One draws on the patterns of vernacular architecture and the other on Shilpaic treatises. Of the first group, some architects based their work on an understanding of the principles that shaped vernacular forms, the result being a unique Modern Indian Architecture. But some were simply entranced by vernacular forms or construction processes—the Vernacularists. The Vernacularists were revivalists whom I will consider later. The concern here is with those who used Vernacular ideas anew or simply found that the answers to modern problems coincided with those of the past. Chronologically, the self-conscious revival of interest in the canonical texts such as the Shilpa Shastras is equally recent. Although the reliance on the ancient shastras had never disappeared from the Indian scene, it was mainly the masons, not architects, and primarily in the south that the ancient Shilpaic traditions had been continued.

MODERN INDIAN ARCHITECTURE

The architects who studied vernacular patterns of architecture during the last quarter of the twentieth century were interested in recognising what those patterns afford that the Modernist ones do not. The studies have led to an understanding of the way buildings were sited, how light and shade were handled, the nature and use of materials and the construction processes employed. The geometries of massing and the symbolic use of decorative elements were also studied. At the Sir J.J. School, Claude Batley had stressed coming to an understanding of the 'inner meanings of old forms and their original functions' (Ghosh, 1998). Some of the recent examinations have indeed penetrated deep into the psyche of architects (e.g., Bhatia, 1994b).

To northern Indian architects, the old towns of Rajasthan, such as Jaisalmer and Udaipur, have been a particular source of inspiration. They possess the visually intricate patterns, sequential experiences and territorial hierarchies that stand in strong contrast to the imported patterns of Modernist ideologies. It has to be remembered that all these traditional patterns evolved in the pre-automobile era, in a highly stratified society, and that they do not necessarily serve present-day ways of life very well. Many architects, nevertheless, employed traditional relationships between cultural patterns and physical forms in their work, particularly for housing areas.

The list of housing developments that might be regarded as exemplars of the Neo-Traditional is substantial. In Delhi alone, vernacular forms have had an impact on the thinking of Raj Rewal in the French Embassy Staff Quarters (1967–9), the Asiad Village (1980–2; for the Asian Games) and the Sheikh Sarai (1980); the Design Group's Yamuna Housing Society (1973–80); and Charles Correa's design for Tara Housing (1975–8). Outside Delhi as well, there are many examples. They include B.V. Doshi's LIC Township (Bimanagar) (1973–6) in Hyderabad, now much altered by its inhabitants; his unimplemented design for the extension of Jaipur, Vidyadharnagar (1985+) and Raj Rewal's more recent Income Tax Colony housing (1996) in Navi Mumbai. All these schemes are unified in their recognition that 'streets' are the seams for life and not, as Modernist ideology suggested, something to be avoided.

The two hundred unit, four-storey Yamuna Housing Society development is based on a network of short streets likened to the mohallas of north Indian cities. All the units overlook a 'pedestrian street' and have been designed internally with the traditional relationships between rooms in mind. The kitchens are located away from the latrines and the bedrooms have access to half-outdoor sleeping areas for use during the summer. Cross ventilation is provided via vertical air-shafts that also afford the use of desert coolers. There are significant Brutalist overtones to the complex with its terraces punched into the façade giving a pugnacious image (M. Chatterjee, 1985; Bhatt and Scriver, 1990).

Raj Rewal has been a prolific user of patterns from Jaipur and Jaisalmer. They give his work a bold interplay of volumes (Taylor, 1992). The difficulty has been to devise ways of handling cars. The Asiad Village consists of 700 dwelling units (200 housing units and 500 apartments). The complex, like Sheikh Sarai, is based on an internal street pattern with interconnecting inner squares/chowks culminating in a central court that acts as a heart for the whole scheme. About ten percent of the units have entrances on both chowks and pedestrian ways. In Sheikh

Jaisalmer

Sarai, the housing is organised into a series of terraces that decrease in size with the height of the buildings. The cars are parked on the periphery—a super-block concept. What residents tend to do in both schemes is to regard the backs of their houses—that face the parking—as the fronts. The result is that the social control mechanisms implicit in the original type are ignored.

In his design of the National Institute of Immunology (1983+) on the Jawaharlal Nehru University campus in south

The Tara Housing, New Delhi

The LIC Township, Bimanagar, Hyderabad

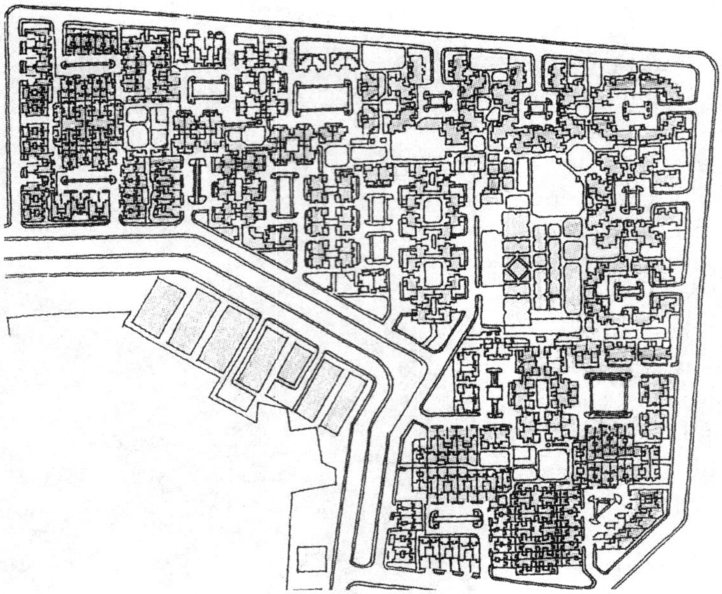

The Asiad Village, New Delhi, plan

The Asiad Village, New Delhi,

Delhi, Rewal continued to be drawn to Rajasthan. In this case it was the *havelis*, and how they handle the climate, that were influential. The step wells of Gujarat were possibly another referent linking the courtyard designs to their Indian roots. In his work of the period Rewal drew on the textures of vernacular built form as the basis for detailing designs rather than the arches, domes and carvings of the referents. A late 1980s housing design for the Central Institute of Educational Technology (1989–90) as well as the Income Tax Colony scheme (1996) show the continuity of Rewal's work. The difficulty throughout arises from the change in scale brought about by the development from the traditional to the modern and the need to provide for the use of cars.

Integrating car usage into a traditional scheme automatically distorts tight-knit urban form types such as the pols of Ahmedabad when they are used as a basis for design today. This impact is clear in the work of Kamal Mangaldas and Devendra Shah in their middle-class suburban housing designs in that city's environs. In the Jai Shefali housing (1979) they created a new residential type with car access, private gardens and such modern amenities as swimming pools. It is only vaguely reminiscent of the pols. Their design for the Gulmohur luxury housing (1986) consists of eighteen units located on each side of a gated avenue of gulmohur trees. The houses are substantial and hearken back to the havelis of Ahmedabad but the colonial bungalow and the way of life it implies may be a closer prototype (Bhatt and Scriver, 1990).

Some of the more interesting examples of this variety of Modern Indian Architecture are institutions. They include the Central Institute of Educational Technology complex itself (1975–88) as well as the National Institute of Immunology, already mentioned, designed by Raj Rewal, and the Indian Institute of Management (IIM, 1977+) in Bangalore designed by B.V. Doshi. Internally they are perceived as environments, externally as objects surrounded by open space.

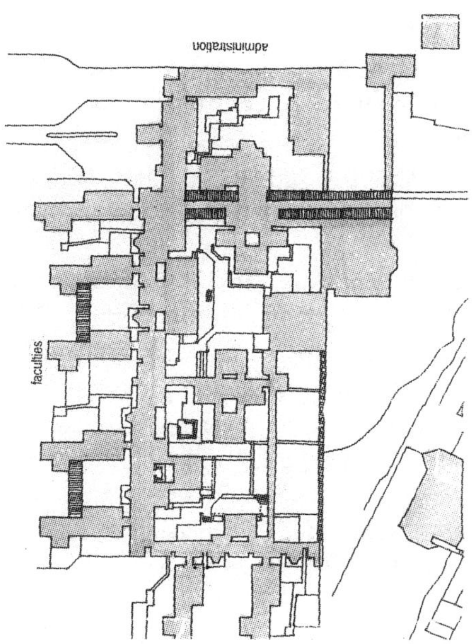

The IIM, Bangalore, plan

The IIM complex consists of a library, extensive lecture and seminar spaces, staff offices and cafeterias, laid out within a framework of broken symmetries around a series of spines, squares and courtyards. This organisation is noted by Doshi as being typical of Fatehpur Sikri (Doshi,

The IIM, Bangalore

1988). In addition, the spines recall the axiality of southern Indian temple galleries. The way in which stone is worked is clearly influenced by Doshi's love of Rajasthani stonework (Bhatt and Scriver, 1990; Bahga, Bahga and Bahga, 1993; Steele, 1998). While the complex has an urban feel to it on the inside, it sits as an independent unit on the periphery of the city.

Deep-seated vernacular ideas also appear in the work of Laurie Baker (b.1917). A Quaker, he has a natural affinity for Gandhian life principles. He worked in the Himalayas when he first arrived in India. There he learnt much about vernacular building forms and construction techniques. He moved to Kerala in 1963 and has worked out of Thiruvananthapuram since 1970. His work, which has become increasingly well known since he won the National Habitat Award in 1987, is within the craft tradition and is possibly the most Gandhian in spirit of all modern Indian architecture.

Baker is against any waste—both of energy consumption and of the materials and building techniques used (Spence, 1980; Baker, 1990; G. Bhatia, 1991; White, 1993). His work stands in strong contrast to the commercial Modern Indian Vernacular work in Kerala with its heavy use of concrete, flat roofs and large picture windows. Baker's links to Modernism are, nevertheless, clear. His concerns for efficiency in circulation, ventilation and the use of light are all within the Functionalist tradition of Modernist work.

The best known example of Baker's work is St John's Cathedral (1973–4) in Tiruvalla. It has a circular plan and is built of local materials: granite piers, brick in-fill panels and brick grill work. The roof is supported on soaring laminated wood trusses; the ceiling is vaulted and the building has dormer windows. Externally, the building is almost Hindu temple-like in appearance. The Centre

St John's Cathedral, Tiruvalla

The Centre for Development Studies, Thiruvananthapuram

for Development Studies (1975) in Thiruvananthapuram has been another influential scheme. It is a complex of brick buildings interspersed with landscaped courtyards and water-bodies. Brick jaalis were used to protect west-facing corridors; openings were carefully placed to aid cross-ventilation. These details of built form enhancing the livability of buildings characterise Baker's work. The Gowarikar House (1982) illustrates his constant effort—this time in domestic work—to reduce costs as much as possible. The brick walls were left unplastered and brick corbelling was used rather than more expensive concrete lintels (Bhatia, 1991).

Uttam Jain's work even more clearly shows links between Modernist and vernacular ideas. His designs for Jodhpur University (1968–79), the Engineering College (1984–91) at Kota, the Balhotra City Hall (1985) and the Neelam Cinema there (1985), all in Rajasthan, the Indira Gandhi Institute of Development Research (1985–7) in Mumbai and the CIDCO (City Industrial Development Corporation) public housing (1988–91) in Navi Mumbai, show a concern for local architectural forms, materials and construction techniques. The Mumbai work shows greater sophistication in material usage and construction techniques simply because the materials are more readily available there and the local craftsmen are familiar with them. What Jain's buildings have in common is the blending of traditional materials and modern expressions (Bhatt and Scriver, 1990; Bahga, Bahga and Bahga, 1993).

The acknowledgment of the importance of such thinking by architectural critics is demonstrated by the Lepers' Hospital (1985) in Chopda Taluka, Maharashtra winning a 1996–8 Aga Khan Award for architecture. Designed by Norwegian architects Per Christian Brynildsen and Jan Olva Jensen, the hospital consists of a series of linear buildings built of slate and steel from Rajasthan, nearby sandstone, bricks made by local villagers, local teak and local lime. Shallow brick vaults are clad with broken glazed tiles recovered from a district factory and coloured tiles top the verandah. While the hospital operates at the cutting-edge of medical knowledge it was almost entirely hand-built.

The Neo-Traditional Architecture described so far has drawn on the indigenous past. There are other vernacular traditions on which architects have drawn. The work in Goa that has inspired Charles Correa and Ralino D'Souza (b.1933), amongst other architects, is the Portuguese colonial. Although Iberian building types have to deal with tropical monsoons in India their reuse in Goan form makes some climatic as well as aesthetic sense. In the Cidade de Goa (1982), a resort hotel in Dona Paula near Panaji, Correa incorporated Portuguese colonial architectural patterns as in the plaza at the entrance, the Mediterranean character of the massing of the overall building and the tiling on the floors. Although some critics see the result as replicating the Goan-Iberian village, it is a highly stylised modern building complex. The Prainha Cottages (1985) designed by D'Souza, in a manner similar to the contemporary work of Ricardo Legoretta (b.1931) in Mexico, is even closer to the Iberian prototype. The massive timber construction, deep

Jodhpur University

The Indira Gandhi Institute of Development Research, Mumbai

verandahs and overhanging eaves of the tiled roof are all reminiscent of Portuguese Goa (Bhatt and Scriver, 1990).

The examples one finds in Pondicherry, where the French colonial work has been an inspiration, lack the thoughtfulness of the work described here. A similar observation can be made about the more pervasive British colonial ideas. Columns

The Cidade de Goa, Dona Paula

and pediments are still used to create the illusion of grandeur. The mundane everyday architecture of the PWDs of the East India Company and later the Presidencies, that could provide lessons to architects even today, is largely neglected. Its utilitarianism lacks the cachet to inspire despite its multi-functionality (Jain, 1991).

The descriptions included here of what fully deserves to be called the Modern Indian Architecture will have to suffice. The list of interesting work could go on and on. Passing mention must, however, be made of Ashish Ganju's Mother and Child Care Centre (1979) in Began, West Bengal, Appukuttam Nair and Narayan Rao's Kalakshestra Theatre in Chennai (1978–84) and Charles Correa's Crafts Museum village cluster (1975+) in New Delhi. They are all fine works completed within one modern approach to design.

The Shastras and Modern Indian Architecture

A number of architects believe that the *Manasara, Mayamatam* and other shastras provide a positive science on which to base architecture in India today. These historical texts provide an array of design principles specifying the location of buildings on their sites, their overall configuration in relation to the social status of their owners, where different facilities should be located as well as providing details of how, for instance, doors and windows should or should not be lined up. The *Vastu-Purusha Mandala* provides the mythological basis for these design principles. The mandala is a square representing the absolute. It can be divided in a number of ways—the basic division being into nine sub-squares. The central square is assigned to the god Brahma while the other squares represent different gods. The application of these ideas today represents a second phase of Modern Indian Architectural work—of looking back to India's spiritual roots. Many architects regard this line of investigation as 'retrogressive'. Certainly, much of the work that is executed in the name of the shastras is simply Revivalist but other examples draw little on past architectural forms *per se.* What all proponents of the Shilpaic traditions do is reject the *basic design* principles invented by the Bauhaus art theoreticians in the 1920s and 1930s (Iengar, 1994, 1996; Devi, 1999). The proposition of the Shilpaic canons is that 'when space . . . is enclosed by the walls of a room, it acquires spiritual properties determined by its shape, size, orientation and location on earth.' The reason is that magnetic energies 'vary with the movement of the sun and influence human beings' (Iengar, 1994).

Mumbai architect, Darshan Kumar Bubbar (b.1937) of Angles Architects has reinterpreted the *Vastu-Parusha Mandala* based on an analysis of the *Manasara* and *Mayamatam* to derive what he argues is an ecologically sound, humanistic basis for modern architectural theory and practice (Bubbar, forthcoming). The buildings that he has designed based on these principles have a modern, indeed Modernist, appearance. The ground floor of his design for the Methodist Centre (1965) in Mumbai was based on the *Chandita Mandala* but the building is utilitarian and also modern in appearance. Its design uses a highly articulated proportional system analogous to Le Corbusier's *Modulor* (Le Corbusier, 1954). Similar observations can be made of Bubbar's other work including the more recent Staff housing and Guesthouse for Berger Paints Ltd (1988–90) in Vallabh Vidyanagar.

The designs of Bubbar and others, such as Keshavram Iengar in Mysore, use the Shastras literally, progressively and thoroughly. They believe the empirical evidence supports their positions. Other architects are less convinced but recognise the importance of this line of investigation. Sensitivities to the shastras are thus found in the work of a number of contemporary architects who come from a strong Modernist background. K.T. Ravindran (b.1947) is an example.

Ravindran's design for the Raghunath house (*c.*1980; with Sanjeeb Chatterjee) displays his Modernist credentials while the building plan is organised according to spiritual demands. It has a central courtyard representing the intangible in the mandala and its construction displays a concern for local traditions. Similarly, in some of his recent work, Charles Correa has attempted to achieve a synthesis of popular culture and an abstracted 'archaic cosmology' (Correa, 1996). The Vidhan Bhavan (1980–93), the Madhya Pradesh capital complex, an Aga Khan Award winner in architecture (1996–8 cycle), is an example. Its layout consists of a complex set of solids and voids within the framework of a nine square mandala in a circular form. The major hall—the most important feature—occupies the central square rather than the traditional open space. While respecting the shastras, Correa exercised an artistic licence within their canons. He took a similar licence in designing the Jawahar Kala Kendra (1986–92) in Jaipur.

The Kendra may well be the best known, internationally, of Correa's recent works. While it is based on a nine square mandala, one square (as in Jaipur city itself) is displaced. In the case of the Kendra, the displacement is more radical than in the city. Unlike the Jaipur plan where a whole square from the northeast has been displaced to the southeast and placed orthogonal to the grid of the remainder of the city, in the Kala Kendra it is only the southeast square that has been displaced. It is also tilted. The materials used for the complex are the same as at

The Methodist Centre, Mumbai

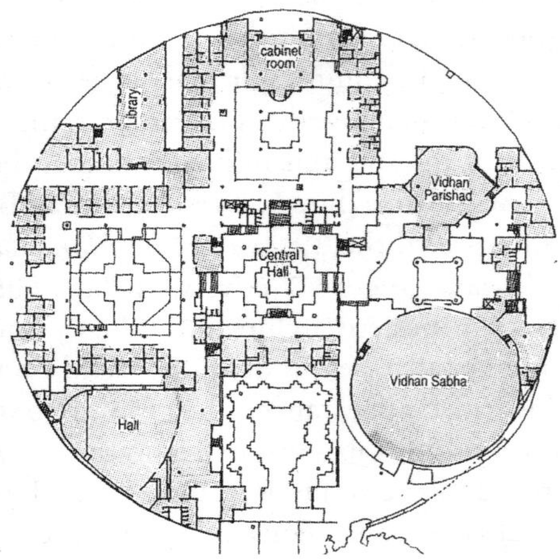

The Vidhan Bhavan, Bhopal, plan

The Vidhan Bhavan, Bhopal

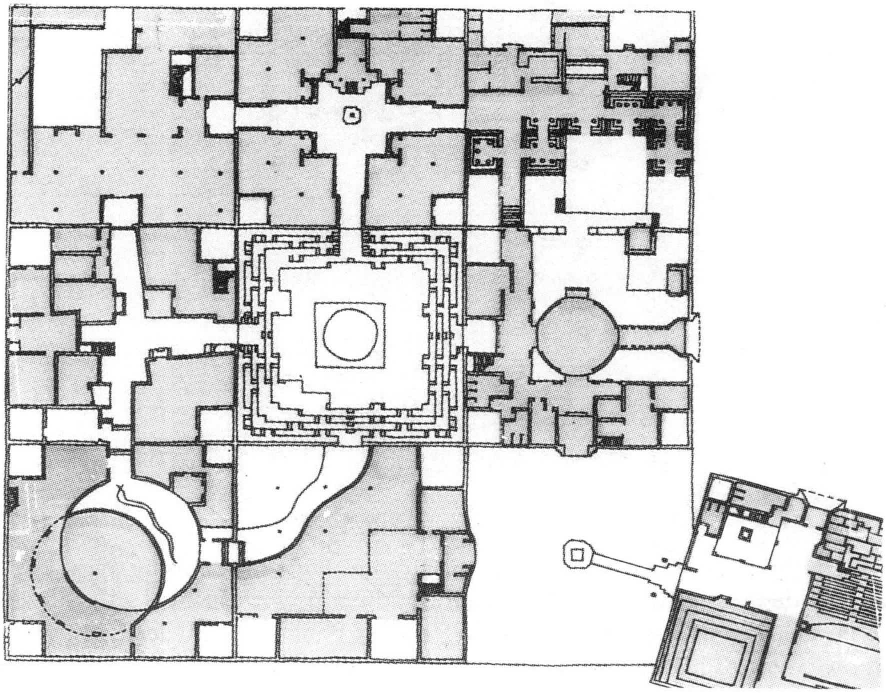

The Jawahar Kala Kendra, Jaipur, plan

The Jawahar Kala Kendra, entrance

The Sumeru Apartments, Mumbai

Fatehpur Sikri and in Jaipur's Jantar Mantar, thus tying the building to its locale. Correa's designs for the British Council Building in New Delhi (1987–92) and the Jawaharlal Nehru Institute of Development Banking in Hyderabad (1986–91) owe more to his seeking 'spaces open to the sky' than to a clear cosmological orientation. More recently (1998), in a project for Bagalkot in northern Karnataka, he has used the mandala as the basis for the plan despite close to half the population being Muslim.

Sen Kapadia is another architect who has looked at the shastras but his analysis of religious referents has focused on different items—colour associations, for instance, rather than the use of the mandala. In the design of the Sumeru Apartments (1993–7), he recognised the cultural and spiritual significance that materials and stones have in India. These meanings are largely lost on the general population but could be revived. Of the gods, Krishna is blue, Shrinath is black; the earth is red and the tulsi plant green and so on. Buildings painted in these colours are not 'just painted buildings, they are enduring symbols of recalled cultural memories' (Ahuja, 1998).

Do these explorations make any sense on other than symbolic grounds relating people to a Hindu heritage? The shastras clearly once had an empirical basis within specific locations. Do they today? Bharat Gandhi is an architect who has found strong links between solar patterns and patterns promulgated by the Vastu Shastra. He has developed computer based software algorithms for evaluating how far a building-design complies with the tenets of that shastra. Today it would, however, seem that the principles on which the canons are founded are more important than the actual canons themselves. Their spiritual basis gives them both authority and authenticity. The future of Shilpaic architecture depends on a broader population embracing the intellectual language of the shastras and so raising their implications beyond that of requiring that half-a-dozen odd patterns be used to sooth old superstitions.

THE VERNACULAR REVIVAL

Vernacular Revival work is a step more basic than the work of Uttam Jain or Laurie Baker although the line between the Neo-Traditional, Vernacular and Revivalism can indeed be blurred. The Vernacularists have, however, been particularly concerned with methods of construction and building.

A number of architects whom one does not usually consider to be Vernacularists have experimented with the vernacular in specific situations. Charles Correa's first architectural commission was the Delhi Handloom Pavilion (1958). It consisted of sixteen squares sitting on an open 'labyrinthian podium' and built of sun-dried bricks. The open spaces were shielded from the sun by sixteen cable-supported parasols with an open square in the centre. Later in his career, in 1975, Correa designed the National Crafts Museum which is a 'village' consisting of a series of buildings and courts—village centre, temple, etc.—based on vernacular types (Khan, 1995; Correa, 1996). Like his Artistes' Village (1983–6) in Navi Mumbai, it will continue to be changed as necessity demands. Despite these examples, Correa can hardly be described as a practitioner of the vernacular although his work shows that he respects it.

The architects in India who might be considered to be practitioners of the vernacular include Rajendra Desai (b.1949) and Rupal Desai (b.1946) from Ahmedabad, Nari Gandhi (1943–93) in Mumbai, K.T. Ravindran and the Kamaths from Delhi. A number of the architects who have explored the use of the vernacular in India are foreign in origin (see Bhatia, 1994a). The focus of attention of architects of the Vernacular has been primarily on the provision of low cost buildings using local labour, materials, and building procedures.

Nari Gandhi, who only completed a dozen odd buildings in his thirty-year career, did his design work on site in much the same manner as the traditional mistri. Most of his work was domestic so he was able to eschew drawings and work directly with craftsmen using the building materials that they knew how to use. Much was left to craftsmen: they could decide what to do and how to do it. The houses, nevertheless, also reflect Gandhi's association with Frank Lloyd Wright.

In his designs Gandhi strove for a sense of the natural and the marvellous, using mythological symbolism. The Sadruddin Daya houses in Versova and Madh Island, Mumbai and the Patel house in Surat show the diversity of Gandhi's work. The Versova house consists of stonework arches, a sloping roof and various textured surfaces while the Patel House uses a controlled, largely orthogonal, geometry. The Versova house nestles in a green, luxuriant compound that penetrates the house's interior and denies its backdrop of high rise buildings.

Possibly the closest a recent architect-designed vernacular building complex that one can come to is the work of Gerard da Cunha (b.1954) at Nrityagram Village (1992+), near Bangalore. This centre for the study of dance, created by Promita Gauri (Bedi), the late Odissi dancer, represents an effort to maintain a way of life and learning. It was built using traditional building forms and

The Artistes' Village, Navi Mumbai (1986)

The Artistes' Village, Navi Mumbai (2000)

The Sadruddin Daya House, Versova, Mumbai

techniques in order to keep both architects and lay people familiar with them. Stone and thatch were the primary materials used. The complex received the award for the best rural architecture from the Vice-President of India in 1991

Nrityagram, Karnataka

The School for Mobile Creches, New Delhi

(Chandavarker, 1991). Nrityagram proved to be neither comfortable nor climatically suitable given contemporary expectations. It has evolved into Kuteeram, a resort hotel, a complex offering much greater comfort for visitors.

In Delhi, Vasant and Revathi Kamath designed buildings showing a similar design philosophy: day-care centres in Dakshinpuri and Seemapuri (1982) and the School for Mobile Creches (1981–3). In form, the school consists of a number of squares and courtyards. It has domes, constructed without shuttering, brick tiles and sandstone elements. They have also designed a number of farm houses—retreats for the urban wealthy—within vernacular traditions, making them unlike most such buildings. Most have been built in a style that has already been introduced, the Modern Indian Vernacular.

THE MODERN INDIAN VERNACULAR

The Modern Indian Vernacular is the architecture of popular middle-class taste. To most academic architects, its exuberance and the eclecticism of its mixture of components is an anathema. They find the mishmash of styles in these buildings deplorable. The results have been dismissed as 'kitsch', something that arises when genuine emotion becomes debased. Yet the work is extraordinarily widespread and should not be lightly dismissed.

The Modern Indian Vernacular is an architecture of display. There are two basic types. The first consists of elements from India's architectural past be it Hindu, Islamic or colonial; and the second is a modernesque form. This latter form is a mixture, not an amalgam, of glass and other shiny materials—marble, polished granite and metals. Often the two types are integrated into what might be called a 'Las Vegas modern'.

Modern Indian Vernacular houses have become an important part of most large and medium sized Indian cities. Plotted houses in areas such as Greater Kailash and other parts of South Delhi, Salt Lake City on the periphery of Calcutta and parts of the Jayanagars in Bangalore exemplify this work. The houses typically

Houses, Greater Kailash, Delhi

have sloping concrete chhajjas, concrete balustrades, projections at floor or parapet level and pitched Mangalore-tiled roofs. Some even have large picture windows facing directly into the western sun. The image sought varies considerably from house to house. Some are neo-Italian Renaissance, others have British colonial antecedents and yet others look back at a host of Indian traditions. Gautam Bhatia (1994a) sarcastically refers to the styles as Punjabi Baroque, Bania Gothic, Early Hardwar, Marwari Mannerism, Sindhi Hacienda, and Anglo-Indian Rococo.

Prior to 1980, the interiors of houses tended to be conservative in plan. Even the nouveau-riche were modest in displaying their wealth. Over time, the ways of day-to-day

Naimesh Park, Ahmedabad

life of the middle class might, with increasing wealth, be said to have become more modern and, certainly, more consumer-oriented. Cooking came to be done standing up in kitchens fitted with counters or platforms, and bedrooms became allocated to specific members of the family. Many houses of Hindu owners, particularly in south India, were and still are, however, being designed with their openings—doors and windows—leading one from the other in a straight line (*nerkuthu*) and with a puja room.

Some architectural work goes well beyond the intellectual level of design of the plotted houses. The Naimesh Park housing project (1984–6) in Ahmedabad seems to owe a debt to Le Corbusier's 1934 design for Algiers (Le Corbusier, 1963). This high-rise, 'Bungalows in the Sky' scheme designed by Yashwant Mistri is an extraordinary deviation from the norm. Another building which has a certain intellectual resemblance to it, is the Ffort, a Radisson Group resort complex (1991–6) at Roychowk near Calcutta. There the architect, Probir Mitra (b.1933), recreated a British naval fort that seems to be a mixture of Modernist patterns and folk-architecture. Although the building is constructed of two hundred year old recycled bricks, its use of brickwork is highly varied as is the building in overall form and detailing.

Dotting the landscape of Indian cities, especially the fast growing centres of Ahmedabad, Bangalore and Mumbai, are an increasing number of high-rise commercial buildings which can certainly be included in the category of Modern Indian Vernacular. They borrow a variety of ideas from a number of past antecedents, including the Classical-Revival. Many are, in Robert Venturi's terms, 'decorated sheds'—standard buildings with stylised skins facing the street (Venturi, 1966). The Mittal Tower (1988) and the Vayudoot Chambers (1993–4), both in Bangalore, are examples of well-executed Post-Modernist designs of this genre. The façades are pastiches but the basic plans are efficient in the best Modernist tradition.

Hafeez Contractor (b.1950), a Mumbai architect, is the major exponent of the Modern Indian Vernacular in his housing designs for builder/developers. In this type of work, in comparison to his other work which ranges from pure Modernist to the Vernacular, Contractor believes that architects are so constrained by by-laws, floor area ratio demands and open space requirements that they are reduced to being little more than exterior decorators (Contractor, 2000). He has executed an extraordinary array of buildings of this type that are clearly much sought after and much loved by many. The developer's world is one of tall towers covered with domes and decorations drawn from ideas around the world. Such designs are easy to denigrate and have been by other architects but they are leaving their imprint on Mumbai as much as the earlier Gothic architecture! The architectural profession around the world has failed to come to grips with this type of demand and certainly, the architectural profession has presented no real alternatives that capture developers' imaginations.

Vayudoot Chambers, Bangalore

Seawood Estates, Navi Mumbai

The facade of Peregrine (1992–5), a building for the Tatas in Prabhadevi, Mumbai, consists of a variety of forms, triangular projections and decorative knots. The Hiranandani Gardens (1987+) in Powai illustrates Contractor's use of domes, pillars and pediments. His designs for the Seawoods Estates (1995) in Navi Mumbai and Beverley Park (1992–5) in Delhi are consumerist designs to the hilt while the Plaza Towers (1996–8) in Gurgaon, Delhi is in comparison, but only in comparison, simple. Contractor is by no means unique in producing this type of work. There are buildings in cities across India that could pass for his designs. His work for builders and developers meet the desires of the wealthy. But much of India needs architects who work at the other end of the economic scale.

THE COMMUNITY ARCHITECTURE MOVEMENT

Many sincere efforts have been made in India to improve housing conditions for the vast numbers of the poor, particularly the urban poor. These efforts date back to the nineteenth century but the major thrusts have occurred since Independence. Various public authorities have built a large number of housing units in Utilitarian Modern designs that have had varying degrees of success in achieving their goals. The 'Sites and Services' approach heavily promulgated in the 1970s was seen to be the modern response to the limitations of the design ideas and financial resources available for low-cost standard social housing. The best known and, possibly, the most successful example of the type in India is Arumbakkam in Chennai.

Developed by the erstwhile Madras Metropolitan Development Authority during the decade 1970–80, Arumbakkam consisted of social facilities (nurseries, primary schools, and clinics), roads and serviced building sites. Sanitary cores (latrine and water supply) were provided for each dwelling unit that was to be built by its owners. This core of facilities was originally placed at the back of the sites but was brought forward to reduce costs and to help with the territorial control residents wished to exert over their plots. Open space in front of the units was originally provided to create a social space but the concept was soon abandoned because the open space was immediately colonised by encroachments. As the residents were responsible for constructing their own houses the designs vary considerably in nature. While hardly a failure, the sites and services approach, as the Arumbakkam experience showed, had limitations. To start with there was a tendency for people allocated sites to soon sell out and move on with some cash in hand. Such attitudes largely defeated the purposes of the whole endeavour.

There has been no Community Architecture Movement *per se.* Disparate groups—mainly non-government organisations (NGOs)—and individuals have a noble advocacy in common: better lives for the poor. The work might be classified as Vernacular but it is modern in that it seeks, if not new products, a new way of delivering them. As the rubric suggests, the primary commonality of all these efforts has been the extensive participation of end users and inhabitants in the design, and often, the construction of the places that they will ultimately inhabit. Activists evolved a number of procedural design principles that were described by Sanjay Prakash as follows:

> the use of trial and error; the participation of users in designing and construction; the participation of workers [as distinct from users] in the entire decision-making process, the multi-disciplinarity [of design consultants]; developing informal rules and procedures in a hierarchy of control; using variety generating building systems or methods [and] creatively using a piecemeal approach to keep future options open to permit course correction (S. Prakash, 1989).

One of the better known of these projects amongst architects is the Vasna Integrated Urban Development Project (1970–5) by the Ahmedabad Study Action Group [ASAG] under the leadership of Kirtee Shah (b.1943) for the Ahmedabad Municipal Corporation. In 1973 floods displaced about twelve thousand people living in villages that were in the dry bed of the Sabarmati River that flows through the city. A somewhat removed site (seven kilometres from Ahmedabad) was donated for their resettlement. ASAG based its design for the settlement on the results of past cases, observational analysis of similar settlements and community feedback. Attention was paid not only to designing for people's activities within dwellings but to the outdoor spaces because in the low-income areas of cities and villages, life spills from the dwelling unit out onto surrounding areas. Models were used to help those involved to understand what the designs would be like. Some people built their own houses but most were erected by construction workers and soon began to be adapted by their residents (K. Shah,

Sites and Services houses, Chennai, 1980

1988). The problem with the project was simply that it is too far removed from potential locations of work. Many of the residents have thus drifted back to their old locations in the riverbed. Nevertheless, Vasna has provided many lessons for other groups.

Architect S.K. Das worked with the project administrator of the Subarkantha Resettlement Project [SRP] to enable the construction of dwellings to be self-managed. The design process recognised the educative role of the architect but in doing so avoided the 'give-them-what-I-think-they-should-have' attitude on the part of those leading the project. Architects presented new ideas to the residents who, in turn, presented the architects ideas new to them (S.K. Das 1991). If architecture can learn from its vernacular past, architects can learn much from vernacular people.

The ideas of the community design advocates have been applied not only to new settlements but also to the upgrading of existing slums. These efforts have involved architects but often it is people from within the community that have led them. Ganeshnagar is still a poverty stricken neighbourhood of about twelve hundred people in Pune, Maharashtra, but the project there (1977–83) led by the sisters Meera Bapat and Sheela Bapat of CDSA has been successful in bringing about both social and physical change by obtaining essential services for the people from local authorities (Mohandas, 1988). It is this type of 'designing' that promises much in poverty-stricken areas.

A REFLECTION

Post-Modernist architects rediscovered the need to understand the links between the problems in India and physical solutions. Ways of thinking about architecture that developed during the twentieth century and endured throughout were those that provided long term solutions to new problems as they arose. Particularly difficult for architects was dealing with the emerging consumer economy and people's needs for what economists call 'positional goods'—those that give identity to a corporation's, institution's or an individual's status in society. Selling a new geometry (i.e., architectural form or pattern) that meets these needs yet fails to solve old problems such as dealing with the climate may be easy in the short run but it has created and will create problems in the longer term.

Looking at and understanding vernacular traditions is a highly educative process because the relationship between context (social and geographic), the building materials available, cultural patterns and aesthetic values, tends to be pronounced. Architects, however, need to avoid falling in love with the forms *per se.* Vernacular building patterns evolved over time in a world very different from that which we inhabit today. Today's world and, perhaps, images of tomorrow's need to guide us.

As the architectural profession in India matured between 1970 and 1995, the Post-Modernist effort to understand the design issues in the country intensified. The need to adopt the styles being developed abroad in order to be seen as *modern* decreased. Thus a number of new approaches to design emerged. Such efforts parallel those elsewhere in the world because, at a generic level, the architectural problems of India are not unique. Their specific solutions may be.

The Torrent Research Centre, near Ahmedabad

7

Searching for Appropriate Architectures: 1985 to 2000

It is difficult enough even with the advantage of hindsight to describe what has happened in the architectural world. Describing our contemporary world is hazardous. Time will yield a better understanding of what was occurring in India at the very end of the twentieth century than a present statement can offer. Some of the approaches to architecture and the architects mentioned here will have been long forgotten and others unnoticed here will have been found to have played a significant role in the development of the discipline and profession.

Much of the recent discussion about architecture has been shaped by literary criticism in which buildings are regarded as texts, open to interpretation. The perception is that we live in turbulent times, therefore the architecture must match. How much has such thinking really affected architectural production? In India? Anywhere? Much has been written and continues to be written about the search for an appropriate Indian architecture as if there were some single Holy Grail to be found (Ameen, 1997). Such a search is futile; obviously there are many grails, each of value in its own right. There can be no single architectural paradigm.

Many of the questions that are being raised about directions in which architectural design should go originated decades ago. The Indian architectural world was small in 1930. It no longer is. At the beginning of this story, there were, perhaps, three hundred architects working in India. Today, there may well be thirty thousand and the number grows. Faced with a changing world, the rise of nationalism on one hand and the pull of the global enterprise and the academic desire to intellectualise architecture on others (assuming one has more than two hands), Indian architects have been increasingly going their own ways.

The search for fresh directions is led by a new generation of architectural philosophers, educators, practitioners and activists located in many different cities. They are closely in touch with their own localities. Their searches take them in different directions because they address different problems. They are inclusive rather than exclusive and more tolerant of ambiguities than many of their predecessors. But then, many of their predecessors have broadened their outlooks and are now amongst them.

At the end of the twentieth century, architecture in India followed a number of coexisting strands of thought addressing different concerns. The results include buildings which exhibit: 1) Modernist principles, ideas and directions including the view that architecture is a pure fine art; 2) minor flirtations with Deconstruction; 3) Neo-Traditional underpinnings; 4) Post-Modernist exuberance, and 5) community involvement. The foci of attention that also came to the forefront during the 1990s were: 1) a greater concern for past architectural and urban forms with much conservation and preservation work, and, increasingly, 2) an 'ecological' architecture. The co-existence of these approaches has enriched the Indian architectural scene and Indian life. Lurking behind these efforts is the question of what an era shaped by information technology development might signify.

CONTINUING TRENDS

Architecture evolves slowly with new paradigms only occasionally emerging. The first four decades of post-Independence architecture in India witnessed several lines of investigation and design. They are likely to persist well into the future. Modernist buildings in their variety of forms will continue to be built, as will Post-Modernist ones. Architects will continue to build on empirical observations. Community architecture must also persist if architects are to be engaged in addressing the full range of problems facing contemporary India.

Modernist Architecture

The architectural ideas that were developed during the first half of the twentieth century have proven to be extraordinarily powerful. There are two continuing overlapping lines of Modernist work: the purist, and the sculptural. They have to seen against the backdrop of the still highly prevalent Utilitarian Modernist work.

In capital outlay terms, buildings—apartments, commercial establishments, houses and housing, and institutional buildings—designed in the Utilitarian Modernist manner are comparatively inexpensive. The use of stucco enables an architect to achieve a smooth finish covering up poor workmanship, and the lack of decorative features enables a modern look to be achieved. Moreover, the relatively simple formula of a concrete slab and beam construction with in-fill panels and strip or punctured fenestration enables buildings to be erected rapidly.

As architects have employed the type for the past forty years, the age of a building is indicated by its state of wear not its design character. Patching and repainting modernises the building again. Such buildings serve a purpose and they are often a pleasant contrast to the more aggressive, attention seeking work that also abounds. If the flamboyant designs of the 1980s and 1990s were a response to the boringness of much utilitarian work then the revival of Modernist architecture has been a reaction to both.

Purist Modernist Architecture

It is not surprising that some architects are looking at the purist phase of Modernist architecture anew. The simplicity of form, the interpenetration of spaces, the precision of detailing and the high level of craftsmanship are an attractive alternative to florid current work. Much has been written about the failures of Modernist architecture; its utility also needs to be recognised.

There are buildings erected during the 1990s that display a simple Modernist touch. The Student Activities Centre at the Indian Institute of Technology in Chennai (1990s) designed by C.K. Raghavendran of the C.N. Narayana Rao office is one example. The building consists of an auditorium and indoor sports stadium. The use of pre-stressed, cast in-situ concrete girders and slab enables free space to be achieved. Simple in external form, the building is functional in its operation and structure.

One of Bimal Patel's recent designs, in particular, raises images of the purist phase of Modern architecture going back to Gropius and Le Corbusier during the 1920s and 1930s. The design is for the Ahmedabad Management Association [AMA], an organisation that provides continuing educational programs and runs conferences. The building is a reinforced concrete block entered by a gentle ramp leading to the entrance hall. The hall has corridors running off it to two wings—one for classrooms and the other for administration and boardrooms. The interpenetration of spaces and the precision of detailing show a revival of interest in the best Modernist architecture. It is also a building much liked by its users. The same can be said for the Gujarat Research Society's School in Khar, Mumbai. Highly functionalist but with a humane touch, it echoes 1930s Rationalist forms though it is an Empiricist building responding to the needs of its users.

What these three examples, the IIT Student Activities Centre, the AMA building and the Gujarat Research Society's school, show is that Modernist architectural forms are still appropriate in context. They are not universal solutions and should never have been touted as such. The number of strictly Modernist buildings being designed in India should not be exaggerated. The Neo-Modernist work is considerably more prevalent.

The Students' Activity Centre, Indian Institute of Technology, Chennai

The Gujarat Research Society's School at Khar, Mumbai

The Ahmedabad Management Association Building

View of the interior, Ahmedabad Management Association Building

Neo-Modernist Architecture

Modernist architectural patterns worked over to be visually more exciting continue to inform the mainstream work of a number of architects in India. This updating is sometimes a response to climatic requirements but often it is a response, in a functionalist manner, to new types of uses that buildings have to serve, and sometimes, to aesthetic whims. There are firms spread across India working in a highly competent, often totally unsung manner, bringing fine buildings to fruition. In Ahmedabad, it is the work of Bimal Patel amongst others; in Calcutta, Dulal Mukherjee; in Mumbai, Somaya and Kalappa, Charles Correa and RMA (Rahul Mehrotra Associates); in Bangalore, Chandavarker and Thacker; in Chennai, K.S. Ranganath and Vergis Oommen. There are many others in every city. A totally different list of names could be just as representative.

Other than the AMA building, Bimal Patel's recent work really falls into the Neo-Modernist classification. It builds on his design for the Entrepreneurship Development Institute [EDI] and includes the Gujarat High Court (1996–7) near Sola, the unbuilt Information Management Resource Centre [IMRC] (1997+) on Kovalam Beach near Thiruvananthapuram and the JMC House (1995–7) in Ahmedabad.

The High Court consists of a number of buildings organised into a campus. The complex is entered through a number of gates, two of which are ceremonial. The central building contains the courtrooms while other buildings house the judges' facilities and various offices. The IMRC was designed to house research and development and allied facilities as well as residences for a management firm employing about a thousand people (Paradkar, 1998). What the two complexes have in common is a simplicity of formal geometry and a concern for patterning light and shade. The overall impression in terms of massing, materials, solids and voids links the designs to their Modernist heritage.

The JMC House was designed as a speculative eleven-storey condominium office building. The building is a simple box that maximises saleable floor area. The façades are divided into vertical shafts of square panels that consist of large champagne coloured glazed surfaces with opaque-glass square centres. Parking is primarily in the basement. The building, in true Modernist fashion, stands as an object in space.

Amongst the architects in south India whose designs are Modernist in their purity of line is K.S. Ranganath (b.1961). Ranganath feels that buildings should have 'a connective link between space, enclosure, light, texture and colour, very much as in a miniature' (R. Shah, 1997). The use of basic forms, pyramids, triangles and vaults and the use of bright colours dominate his work. His design for his cousin's house in the Cholamandal Artists Village achieves a sculptural form using curving lines. Openings are kept to a minimum. His design of a colony of houses for Madras Fertilisers Ltd at the Manali industrial area is a veritable collection of basic forms that add up to a lively communal environment.

The Housing Colony for Madras Fertilisers, Ltd, Chennai

The current work of the Mumbai firm of Somaya and Kalappa (in reality, Brinda Somaya), one of the small but growing group of women-headed practices in India, can clearly be described as Neo-Modernist. Somaya's work ranges from industrial buildings (TEDS, 1987) and housing (Wartsila Housing, 1994), to houses (Garware House in Nasik, 1986; a winner of an Indian Institute of Architects award in 1994) and commercial buildings (Brady Gladys Plaza, 1998) as well as corporate headquarters (Gokaldas Images, Bangalore 1998). This body of work is characterised by the simplicity that Modernists seek but also has free-flowing lines and a visual richness that they missed. Although it uses very different patterns, this search for spatial and visual richness can also be seen in houses such as that for Anil Patel (1999) in Vadodara designed by Anand M. Shirgaokar. In this case the basic forms extend as sculpture into the surrounding landscape.

Although it has vernacular overtones, the Sanskriti Kendra (1990–3) in Anandgram, Delhi, designed by Upalghosh Associates is really a Modernist venture. The Kendra, spread over three hectares, is home to a number of art and cultural endeavours, traditional and modern. The complex consists of the Baithak, the common room of the Kendra, a haveli, two studio blocks, two museums and a 'village complex' for rural crafts. The village has a courtyard with a *kund* and a pigeon coop. The buildings are constructed predominantly of reinforced concrete and brick and painted brown to fit into the environment. The buildings sit as objects within a landscape designed in the English Landscape tradition by

The Garware House, Nasik

The Anil Patel House, Vadodara

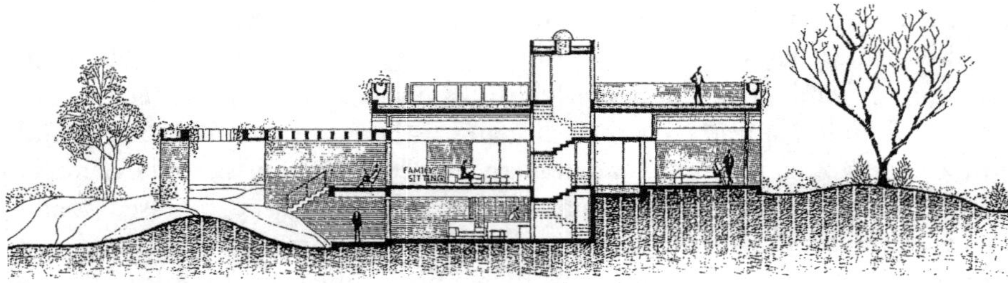

The Anil Patel House, longitudinal section

Mohammed Shaheer. A rainwater channel converted into a rivulet and pools, picks up Indian traditional concepts.

A building with a very different appearance, but within the same design idiom, is that for Infosys (1993–4), a software firm, one of many in Bangalore. A detailed brief that described how the firm actually operates, not its formal structure, guided the design. In addition, the client sought an unpretentious building. Prem Chandavarkar of Chandavarkar and Thacker designed an introverted complex of two major blocks—one is the major working area and the other provides supportive services. An atrium roofed with a filler slab (also much used by Laurie Baker) runs the length of one wing giving views to the central space. A low 'bridge' over a storm water run-off channel that ends in a recharge pond connects the two wings. The area has been landscaped to form a central green area for the campus.

The Sanskriti Kendra, Delhi

The grid appearance of the building is characteristically Neo-Modernist. It is very much a function of the demands of the technology used and workstation-sized modules. Grooved concrete blocks have been built up into columns with granite slabs (*chapdi*) fitted into the grooves to form walls. The pointing is raised, and raised granite slabs form lintels and sills. The materials of the façade are left exposed while the interiors of the walls are brick-lined and plastered. What is obtained is a simple, highly functional building with livable interiors.

A Note on Neo-Modernist Interior Architecture

Interior architecture is gathering increasing professional recognition. Much of the everyday work of internationally renowned architectural firms such as that of Cesar Pelli (b.1926)—indeed the work that enables them to spend extra time (and money) on award winning architecture—is the design of the interiors of buildings. It is seldom-celebrated work yet very important in an era of apparent rapid reorganisation of commercial firms.

Some of the outstanding Neo-Modernist work in India during the 1990s was in interior design. Somaya and Kalappa's designs for The Hong Kong and Shanghai Banking Corporation and Leela Scottish Lace Pvt., Ltd. both show a simplicity of surfaces but with the considerable added warmth in colour and decoration that distinguishes Neo-Modernist work from both Purist and the recent 'glitzy' Post- Modernist design.

The interior, RMA Offices, Mumbai

The interior architecture work of Rahul Mehrotra and his colleagues at Rahul Mehrotra Associates (RMA) is similar in attitude. In Maruwala House (1988), the minimalist approach to interiors—the framing of views, the punching of windows into the laterite walls and the simplicity of the interiors—shows the Modernist spirit. The richness of materials and colours and, externally, the sloping roofs and large verandahs all show a departure from the strict Modernist vocabulary. The same character appears in the design of the firm's own offices (1997) in Mumbai and in the design of commercial interiors such as that for Bandhej (1997), a store in Ahmedabad dealing with textiles and accessories. The use of small window openings to link spaces and the variety of materials used display a different spirit from the functionalist interiors of, say, the Indore Palace of the 1930s designed under Eckhart Muthesius' direction.

The amount of neo-Modernist work in India is vast. What is being increasingly recognised is that the quality of life of people (to the extent that it is shaped by the built environment) probably depends more on the qualities of the interior space than of any other aspect of built form. While some of the recent work has a sculptural quality to it, it is not presented as sculpture. But some buildings really are.

Architecture as an Art Form, as Sculpture

In response to all the utilitarian work around them, architects sometimes seek a more free-form expressive architecture. The buildings at Auroville have already been mentioned. Such sculptural forms are easier to attain in some building types than in others. First of all they tend to be freestanding. True Antonio Gaudi (1852–1926) in the Casa Milá in Barcelona (1905–10) and Frank Lloyd Wright in the Guggenheim Museum (designed 1943–6) achieve buildings of extraordinary, although very different, sculptural qualities. Both, however, are corner sites. Gaudi's building is also unusual in that it was a substantial residential building; museums are more typical opportunities to display flair as Frank Gehry (b.1929) has done with the Guggenheim Museum (1994–6) in Bilbao, Spain.

What differentiates the contemporary Indian sculptural efforts from the Museum in Bilbao is that they take on a magical-realism. Gehry's work can be seen as an extension of the Bauhaus 'Basic Design' course and is the logical next step in free-form to Le Corbusier's chapel at Ronchamp (1950–4). In India, the art is spiced—figuratively—with narratives of fantastic ideas and forms. This link is most apparent in the Hussain-Doshi Gufa (1992–5), popularly known as Amdavad ni Gufa, on the grounds of CEPT in Ahmedabad.

Sun City, outside Calcutta, designed by Development Consultants, as well as some of Nari Gandhi's or Gerard da Cunha's works have a sculptural qualities, and Dean d'Cruz uses playful forms in his houses and resorts; but it is the Gufa that best illustrates the fuzzy border between building and fine arts. Seeing the

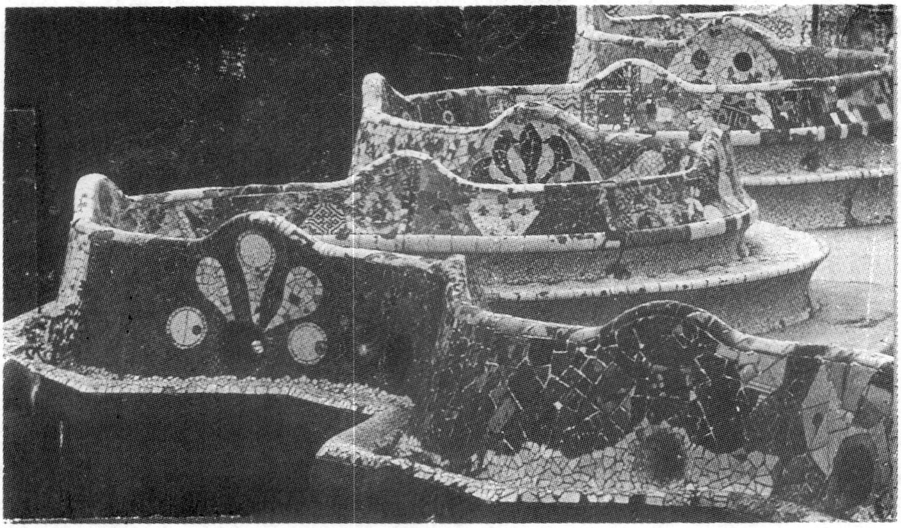

Parc Güell, Barcelona

The Hussain-Doshi Gufa, Ahmedabad with the Gujarat University Tower in the background

Hussain-Doshi Gufa in terms of Gaudi's Parc Güell (1900–14) in Barcelona, with which it has visual similarities, makes little sense. The Gufa is a semi-underground, cave-like gallery for the display of art works, primarily those by M.F. Hussain, but it is itself as much a display as anything within it. Its specific location is based on Doshi's divination and its free-form domical exterior and 'treed' columnar interior is spiritually inspired. 'The references for the Gufa are primeval: the cave, the circle, the mountain, the breast . . . the Buddhist stupa' (Steele, 1998). The latter form has been considerably abstracted and is a thin shell punctured with projecting circular skylights—'snouts'—to illuminate the cave below. The building is a passionate expression similar to that of Le Corbusier, at Ronchamp. There, implicitly if not explicitly, Le Corbusier gave free rein to his feelings about Catholicism's attitudes, positive and negative, towards spirituality and sexuality. Certainly the design of the Gufa coincides with Doshi's broader use of narratives—stories—to shape and explain his designs.

If in the Gufa Doshi was seeking spiritual congruence with ancient India, the architects of the Neo-Traditional were concerned with more down-to-earth issues.

Neo-Traditional Architecture—The Modern Indian Architecture

Vernacular buildings and settlements allow us to understand better the relationships amongst built forms, human activities and aesthetic values. They have also been studied as a means of identifying what *our* architecture looks like, region by region. What emerged from the application of the insights drawn from these studies, it was suggested in the last chapter, is a unique modern Indian architecture. An understanding of those principles will remain an important source of empirical knowledge about building patterns and what they afford people. The study of past construction methods also became important because of the perceived failure of aspects of Modernist construction work. Thirty years after Le Corbusier and Kahn made concrete and brick fashionable building materials in India, many buildings suffer extensively from concrete cancer—the corroding of steel reinforcing bars that were laid too close to the concrete's surface and the subsequent crumbling of the concrete—and from excessive efflorescence of the exposed brickwork.

By the year 2000 four stages in the development of post-Independence Neo-Traditional architecture could be identified. The first phase had involved a love affair with desert cities such as Jaisalmer. The second looked at the spatial qualities of buildings rather than the forms themselves. The third went back further in history to the Shilpaic traditions. Architects then started to use narratives based on fables to create or perhaps justify their designs as in the National Institute of Fashion Technology (1997) in New Delhi designed by Doshi. Work representing all these phases continues to be built but a number of lessons have been learnt from the experiences of the 1970s and 1980s.

One thing that da Cunha learnt in designing Nrityagram is that simply aping the vernacular no longer suffices. Nisha's Play School in Goa builds on his experience with Nrityagram. He has been careful to allow for the free flow of air from room to room. The building, built of brick, laterite stone, thermacole, china mosaic, bottles and stained glass, is rich in colour and form. It is full of fun for children and is entirely modern yet its aesthetic is drawn from the vernacular experience. There are many permutations of such attitudes in contemporary designing.

B.S. Bhoosan (b.1946), working out of Mysore, seeks an architecture 'for the common man' learning from the past but simultaneously recognising that new ways of life are being sought and new technologies often serve people better than the old. In his social housing designs, Bhoosan has attempted to base designs on the cluster and row house developments of the past but he finds public agencies resistant to changing their norms (Bhoosan, 2000). His original design for a mixed-income HUDCO-aided project on a wedge-shaped ten-acre (four-hectare) site created sets of neighbourhoods through the clustering of housing around common spaces. At the core of the whole development would be central facilities. The design recognised that the quality of life of low-income populations depends on the quality of the infrastructure as much as on the quality of the housing units. The public authorities found it more important to get units built than to have thoughtfully designed open spaces as well. The project has ended up being conventional. The question of what is acceptable behaviourally and symbolically to whom remains at the core of architectural debates.

The work of Ahmedabad-based Kulbhushan and Minakshi Jain addresses the problem of what is symbolically appropriate. Courtyards in houses make climatic sense in much of India but the courtyard house is a type that is often regarded as 'old-fashioned'. The Jains have found that terraces are symbolically acceptable as modern in lieu of courtyards. The Kothari house (1985–6) that they designed is double storeyed, entered on the side in front of garages. The downstairs is the quasi-public space of the houses and the first floor is the private family area. A circular stair reaches the bedrooms, studies and the terraces on the floor above. The dining room, as is the tradition, is the central room on the ground floor to which visitors have easy access and from where ground floor activities can be controlled (Pruthi, 1991).

The same effort to deal with modern demands, concepts of up-to-dateness and Indian traditions can be seen in the Mahindra United World College in Pune (1995–8), a village-like complex designed by Christopher Benninger and Associates, a firm based in the city. The heart of the campus is a relatively small quadrangle surrounded by classrooms, each with its own garden into which the activities of classes can spill. Four ramped passages, aligned to the cardinal directions and open to views, radiate from the quadrangle. One of the radiating ramps leads to the entrance that is marked by a *Madhadwarra*, an old wooden gate. On one side of the entrance is the Administration Centre while the Science Centre is on the other. Another passage leads to a multi-purpose hall and the other two to the Catering Centre and to the Arts Centre and Library. Lawns are interspersed

The Kothari House, Ahmedabad

Mahindra United World College, Pune

between the blocks and the toilet blocks exist independently. Four residential clusters, or *wadis*, exist in the form of hamlets of six *wadas*. Five staff homes are organised around a common room and a small amphitheatre. These clusters are

The Sri Sri Radha Parthasarathi Mandir, Delhi

themselves clustered around the amenities for the entire campus. The use of materials—stone and concrete—and the scale of the buildings visually tie the whole complex together. The College shows the impact of vernacular design with its reliance on the *wada* system but it also has similarities to the work of Joseph Stein in the handling of materials and form.

India has seen a considerable religious revival recently. In Hinduism, architecture and religion are closely linked so the detailing of temples is important. The difficulty is to maintain the detailing while designing in a modern manner. The Sri Sri Radha Parthasarathi Mandir (1997–9) designed by Achyut Kanvinde for the International Society for Krishna Consciousness has abstracted traditional forms in an almost Post-Modern manner to indicate the building's place in time and space.

The vernacular is a good teacher. In drawing on the vernacular, modern Indian architecture is often more energy-efficient than the Modernist. Thus much Neo-Traditional work is closely related today, as will be shown later, to the efforts to create an ecological architecture. Deconstructionist attitudes are, in contrast, highly intellectual.

Deconstruction

Deconstruction is perhaps the exemplar of the Post-Modern experience. In literature, it challenges the status quo—the conventions of form and composition. Architects following suit strive for a sense of uneasiness, decentring, dislocation and absurdity (Tschumi, 1988). Deconstruction has, to this point, been so academically bound in its internal philosophical arguments, that it has had little impact on what was built in India during the last decade of the twentieth century. Whether or not it will in the future is open to conjecture.

The Jawaharlal Kala Kendra in Jaipur, designed by Charles Correa, is

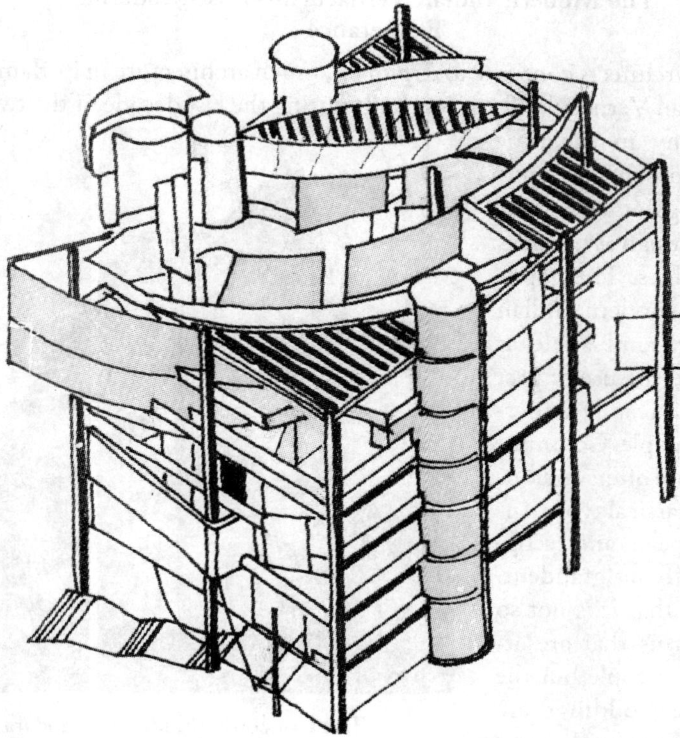

Competition entry, new headquarters building for the
Indian Institute of Architects

sometimes pointed out as an example of deconstructionist thinking. If anything, it is closer in thinking to the work of Post-Modernists such as Robert Venturi in that it uses standard elements from the past in an abstracted manner. Bimal Patel took a similar disjointed liberty in an aspect of his design of the High Court of Gujarat. From the main entrance the apparent symmetrical organisation is misleading. The building opposite is off-centre. What appears to be capricious is a carefully reasoned act (B. Patel, 1999).

Perhaps an inkling of what is in some architects' minds can be seen amongst the competition submissions for the new Indian Institute of Architects Headquarters in Navi Mumbai during the mid-1990s. Some designs showed a striving for formal disjunctions in their presentations to the world. Whether they will set a trend remains unclear. Deconstruction, to make any logical impact on the Indian scene, will require a highly creative compromise between French assumptions (for deconstructionist observations are French at heart) and Indian realities. What is much more likely in professional practice is a continuation, indeed flourishing, of a post-modern exuberance.

The Modern Indian Vernacular—Post-Modern Exuberance

While many architects continue to deplore it, much architecture in its flamboyant Modern Indian Vernacular form was built during the last decade of the twentieth century. Many in the property development community encourage it and their values drive design as much as architects' values. The popularity of the Modern Indian Vernacular was and is due, at least partly, to the use of past forms that are readily understood by lay people. Columns, for instance, are often versions of standard classical types, Indian or European, and recognised as signifying grandeur. One thesis is that it is not so much the forms that are attractive to lay people but the way that the buildings are highly articulated with bases and cornices and their façades divided into components; they have a recognisable organisation (Mehrotra, 1999). Hafeez Contractor continues to be highly productive with the City Bank Complex (1996–8) in Bandra-Kurla being more a Neo-Modernist design than most people associate with him. The building he designed for Colgate Palmolive (India) Limited (1998–9) is typical of his recent work for developers with its pediments and colonnades (Panwani-Talib, 1999, Contractor, 2000).

The Concorde Building, Vadodara

The TSR Towers, Hyderabad

Zacharia and Thomas completed some fine work in

Bangalore as a partnership and apart from them, many new faces have begun to be seen on the architectural scene. One of them is that of architect Sanjay Puri whose work in Vadodara varies from Neo-Modernist simplicity (e.g., Blue Chip, 1990–2) to Post-Modernist liveliness (e.g., the Concorde building, 1997+). Clearly signifying the jet age to a lay audience in much the way that Art Deco signified the age of industrial and ship design, the Concorde building is a composition of lively forms. The base has a central atrium around which shops are located—an increasingly common type in a consumer economy. The office block placed diagonally above has only peripheral columns and the façade above the entrance is entirely of glass. Steel beams protrude and the external columns give 'a jet set appearance'. The remainder of the façade, while simpler, is fragmented in colour, texture and form. In Modernist fashion, the different functions have been clearly articulated (Lohana, 1998).

A more typical example of Post-Modernist exuberance is the TSR Towers scheme in Hyderabad (1995+) designed by Jayashree and Kapil Bhalla of SEARCH. It draws together elements from past architectures and uses modern materials. Like many recent commercial buildings, classical columns are a part of its façade. There are two of them holding up a curved surface with a low dome above. The columns stand on bases between which there is a wrought iron railing. A recess above the ground floor emphasises the entrance. The elements in combination give the building both a sense of grandeur and a human scale.

Community Architecture

A sense of grandeur is not what the community activists seek in their work. Community architectural work of the 1990s included those types that had been developed earlier. If in the 1950s and 1960s the primary concern was with slum clearance and new housing, in the 1970s with sites and services programs, and in the mid-1980s with slum upgrading, during the 1990s it was with slum redevelopment. Incremental improvements in the living conditions of the poor without disrupting the ways of life that make their survival possible continue to be essential in less wealthy economies.

Throughout India, both governmental agencies and non-governmental organisations are involved in the effort to improve the lives of the poor. Amongst such groups, Anita Reddy heads AVAS (Association for Voluntary Action and Services, founded in 1980) in Bangalore; YUVA (Youth for Unity and Voluntary Action, founded in 1985) is active in Mumbai and Nagpur and the activist Gita Balakrishnan is busy in Bangalore. Architects and other design professionals have made substantial contributions to such efforts. Many subsidise community work through more conventional practices.

Tenure over a site remains vital for slum upgrading as a comparison between two sites in Hyderabad—Nirankainagar and Indiranagar—shows. Inhabited by people of remarkably similar income, the amount invested in each community by

Nirankainagar, Hyderabad

Indiranagar, Hyderabad

its residents is very different. In Nirankainagar people believe they have tenure (although not legally) while at Indiranagar, they know they do not (Rao, 2000).

During the 1990s a number of approaches to housing low income groups were tried. They included the provision of subsidised walk-up flats and three storey

Three storey walk-up units, Hyderabad

Borabanda Housing, Hyderabad

beam and slab structures that individual households could fill in to make their own apartment units (e.g., Borabanda housing in Yusufguda, Hyderabad). Fine though such efforts may be, they reach only a minority of low-income people. As a result, much recent work does not involve the building of housing units but simply focuses on the upgrading of the infrastructure of areas as a catalyst for local people to take the initiative to invest in their own properties.

The continuing importance of community architecture work was recognised by the award of an Aga Khan prize for architecture (1996–8 cycle) to Himanshu Parikh, a civil engineer, for his work since 1989 in Indore. The Slum Networking project there was of the scale necessary to deal with the needs of a substantial proportion of India's one billion population. The project reached five lakh people, bringing together governmental agencies, non-government organisations and industries as a coalition to tackle the problems of 183 slums of varying sizes in the city.

The goal was to create a clean living environment by using the multiplier effect of introducing efficient sewerage, storm drainage and fresh water supply systems to a slum environment. The State Government provided householders with long-term leases. As a consequence the slum dwellers were willing to pay for their own toilets and connections to sewers. This action had the added benefit of giving residents territorial control over a piece of land and the security of tenancy that makes it worthwhile for them to improve their own abodes. The use of the catalytic effect of public investment is an important characteristic of urban designing today.

Whether such efforts can be carried out on as vast a scale as India requires remains open to conjecture. Much has to do with the spirit (and stamina) of the people, including architects, involved. A number of architects have found the rewards, psychological and financial, of working with poor communities too limited in comparison with the comparative comforts of conventional practice. They have moved into standard architectural practices carrying what they have learnt (and probably a number of intellectual scars) with them. Others, however, are devoted to working with low-income people.

EMERGING TRENDS

It is somewhat misleading to describe the current concern for the biogenic health of the world and the work in preservation and conservation as emerging trends. Both are of long-standing in India. They date back at least to the work of Patrick Geddes (1854–1932) in Chennai and other cities during the 1920s (Meller, 1977) and, even earlier, to the founding of the Archaeological Survey of India in the nineteenth century. Nevertheless, the concerted broad-scale effort in these areas of architectural practice is recent, as is the concern with the impact of new information technologies on architectural form. How information technology will affect the built environment of the future remains conjectural. Much depends on how ways of life and aesthetic values evolve.

Ecological Architecture

It is hardly surprising that India, with its billion people and continually expanding population, is feeling the consequences of high population densities in both its urban and rural districts. The major cities suffer from high levels of air pollution, many rivers are open sewers and irreplaceable energy resources are being rapidly consumed. People everywhere demand manufactured goods, which means a continuing demand on natural resources and a considerable discharge of waste. Over the next decade, the explorations by architects in India of ways to reduce energy costs in creating and running buildings promise to enhance our knowledge considerably.

The science in this area is still underdeveloped. What is obvious and logical on paper has often proven to be incorrect in the four dimensional world. Designing environmentally suitable buildings and cities does not come easily especially as the symbolic demands people make of the built environment frequently push in the opposite direction. Passive modes of climate control in buildings (i.e., through using natural ventilation via wind walls and windows, vegetation for shadowing and cleaning air, tromp walls, etc.) only yield a marginally more comfortable environment than that achieved in a standard concrete and slab building without air-conditioning. Using artificial heating in winter and air-conditioning in summer is clearly the way to achieve a high level of comfort for people but it is very energy consuming. Mixed modes of heating and cooling are currently being explored. They do require people to trade off comfort levels for energy efficiency (Krishan, 2000).

It is easier to achieve energy efficiency in small-scale homes than in high rise buildings. There has been, as yet, no equivalent in India to the work of Ken Yeang (b.1948) on tall buildings in Malaysia (Yeang, 1996). There are, however, a noteworthy number of ecologically sound buildings in India. Although his recent work is often at an institutional scale (e.g., the Drug Rehabilitation Centre in Pune, 1999), the work of Shirish Beri, for instance, has focused on buildings such as farm houses. His own, Hirvai (1980–3), is a good example.

Hirvai, located on a lush two-hectare site, was built largely of materials excavated on site, and local laterite stone. A large verandah serves both as an entrance and as the principal living space of the house. An orchard and vegetable gardens provide the essential foods of life. Animal and human waste is digested in a biogas plant to provide gas for cooking while effluent provides the fertiliser for the garden (Bhatt and Scriver, 1990). This example is not unique. Similar explorations in their own houses have been made by other architects (e.g., B.S. Bhoosan in his own house in Mysore) and in many villages around India where water conservation is crucial to survival.

Kiran Pandhya has tackled the problem in a factory building, Inductotherm, in Ahmedabad, with some success while the Torrent Research Centre (1997+) by Nimish Patel and Parul Zhaveri of Abhikram is another significant example of

Hirvai, Nadhawade

a larger scale project. It is the more architecturally dramatic of the pair. The Centre, located outside Ahmedabad, is a pharmaceutical research laboratory which, in consultation with Brian Ford Associates of London, has been designed to be climatically responsible. The goal was to have a building that requires minimum maintenance (important in a country where high quality maintenance does not come easily) and be cost effective in the long run.

With its functional divisions, clarity of form and ease of circulation, the plan is strictly Modernist. Although there is central air-conditioning for laboratories, towering ventilation shafts enable a down-draft evaporation system for cooling to be used for other facilities. Simple devices such as cavity walls and the lack of openings on the east and west façades enhance the ambient temperature quality within the building. How successful is the result? The temperature inside can be as low as 30°C during the summer when the outside temperature is in the 40s. At that time between six and nine air changes—in which the total volume of air in a room is replaced by another volume of air—are obtained per hour. In terms of embodied energy, in the materials and construction methods used in the building, the attempt was made to use local unprocessed materials rather than synthetics (Chauhan, 1998; N. Patel, 2000).

A number of other firms are carrying out similar explorations around India. Gayathri and Namith Shetty designed the Samskrutha Pathashala in Sringeri which lies in the Malnad belt of southwest Karnataka. The complex is built around a large court whose trees were preserved. It is constructed of natural materials using recycled wood from old houses for columns and floors. The roofs are of Mangalore tiles. Manipal House, a corporate office designed by the same firm is a reworked factory building. The use of recycled materials in these buildings reduces the amount of embodied energy in them.

There are a growing number of such explorations both in reworking existing buildings and creating new ones. In the Mysore area, B.S. Bhoosan pioneered the use of discarded wood from fallen coconut trees as well as salvaged materials in building construction. He has used these materials, traditional technologies and Mangalore tiled roofs over wall-less spaces in a number of recent resort and health

Le Olive, Mysore

clinics (e.g., The Village completed in 1997 and Le Olive in 1999). The goal has been to deal with the climate without resorting to expensive cooling devices (Bhoosan, 2000).

Not only has such a concern for energy efficiency been shown in the warm and tropical areas of India but also in areas where the climate is cooler. The new building for the Autonomous Hill Development Council (1996) in Ladakh, designed by Arvind Krishan, has to cope with cold winters and cool summers. Instead of hiding from the sun, the goal there was to use the sun's heat to reduce heating costs (Krishan, 2000).

The issues in designing ecologically sound buildings extend beyond the complex concerns of energy efficiency in both building construction and operation to concerns with how landscapes are considered. The techniques are varied: the reduction of hard surfaces to reduce water run-off, the use of retention ponds to recharge water tables, the use of indigenous types of vegetation to encourage the presence of native birds, etc. These concerns are likely to become much more important in the future at both an architectural and urban design scale. Although not generally considered in the same light, the preservation and conservation efforts of architects has much in common with those of the ecologists.

Preservation and Conservation

The preservation of buildings that are regarded as monuments is primarily the concern of the Archaeological Survey. Its work, of preserving monuments regardless of the personage, race or creed behind them, was given a boost by Lord Curzon

(1859–1925; Viceroy, 1899–1905) at the beginning of the twentieth century. INTACH [the Indian National Trust for Architectural and Cultural Heritage] now with a twenty-year history of its own, has been doing the same. As India is extraordinarily rich in its architectural history—Hindu, Islamic and colonial—questions about how best to identify what is important and what is not are difficult to answer. The European and American fabric-oriented focus referring to the physical structure, form and materials of a building when establishing the relevance of artefacts, often misses the symbolic geography of a place.

Urban Arts Commissions setting criteria for establishing what is important and what is not exist in a number of cities. Various other groups such as the Indian Heritage Society in Mumbai (founded 1988), the Bombay (Mumbai) Conservation Group (founded 1990) and Calcutta's Centre for Preservation of Urban Traditional Values have become public interest groups promoting the preservation of not only monuments but, often, everyday buildings. These buildings give a city life and are meaningful to different groups of its inhabitants.

Of large scale concern is the preservation of psychologically important segments of cities where redevelopment would be temptingly profitable financially to developers and corporations. These areas consist of central business districts developed under colonial auspices during the second half of the nineteenth and the first part of the twentieth centuries, and the old (not necessarily older) indigenous parts of cities: the *parras, mohallas, stores*, and *pols*. The cores of cities as diverse as Hyderabad, Aurangabad, and Delhi (Old and New) have undergone great change in recent times both in physical nature and in population. Structures have been demolished to provide access for cars; chowks have been converted into parking areas, and buildings gutted to make way for more 'functional' blocks with façades 'modernised' to be fashionable.

During the 1990s a number of people, including architects and architectural firms, became strongly committed to preservation, conservation and restoration work: Jai Sen in Calcutta; Debashish Naik in Ahmedabad, Rahul Mehrotra Associates and Somaya and Kalappa in Mumbai, the historian, Narayani Gupta, and Nalini Thakur in Delhi, and Avanlika Chitnavis in Nagpur. The list could go on. Some architects are purists in the sense of being concerned only with buildings that have a historical importance (as an architectural style or because some important event or events took place there). Others are advocates for retaining financially less profitable buildings simply because we are incapable of replacing them with new ones of equal merit either because the crafts people are no longer available or, more often, because it is too costly. Yet others favour conservation because of both the embodied energy required to replace buildings and because vernacular and colonial buildings are often energy efficient in comparison with both Modernist work and much of what is being built today. Old buildings are also what lure tourists—an important financial consideration.

During the 1960s and 1970s a number of palaces were converted into internationally renowned five star hotels—the Lake Palace in Udaipur being the best

The Malabari Memorial Hall, Mumbai, before renovation

After renovation

known. The range of work undertaken during the 1990s was remarkable. Calcutta's Town Hall (1813), after falling into severe decay by 1990, was restored to its former splendour (1995–8) under the direction of Dulal Mukherjee and Partha

Das; Debashis Naik had earlier completed the basic groundwork. Buildings such as the Cathedral and John Connor School in Mumbai and the West End Hotel in Bangalore were tenaciously and cautiously upgraded (1992–6) by Brinda Somaya of Somaya and Kalappa to meet contemporary requirements while preserving the old. Somaya was also responsible for the upgrading of Nityanand Ashram in Ganespuri. Encroachments were removed, the temple repainted and the surrounding surfaces paved.

Recently, a few houses of historical note have been brought back to their former glory. They include the Lutyens-designed Kum-Kum bungalow (1935–6) by Abhimanyu Dalal (b.1958) and the 1850 Luz house in Chennai. The Sural mud palace (dating from 1511) near Udipi in coastal Karnataka has been restored under the direction of Vijayanath Shenoy. Buildings of no particular historic note are also being renovated simply because they offer much. The Malabari Memorial Hall (designed by K.P Daver in 1924) of the Seva Sadan Society, for instance, was restored and upgraded under the direction of Harshad Bhatia in early 2000.

Throughout the world, fine nineteenth and early twentieth century industrial buildings have become obsolete as a result of changes in manufacturing and transportation technologies and land tax structures. They are unpretentious buildings, often extremely well constructed, and have a spatial layout that affords many opportunities internally and a sense of urbanness externally. In Lower Parel, Mumbai, for instance, a number of cotton mills are no longer operating and are ripe for redevelopment. Brinda Somaya designed the conversion of the Kamala Mills into an office complex. Shimul Jhaveri Kadri (b.1962), also of Mumbai, converted a warehouse into a corporate office for Synergy (1998). Such conversions are occurring with frequency. They require considerable architectural ingenuity but also provide a freedom of expression in interior architecture.

During the late 1980s and 1990s, there was much documentation of historic buildings. In almost all schools of architecture students have produced fine measured drawings of important monuments and everyday vernacular buildings. Most languish in filing cabinets. Professionals work towards a specific purpose. The UDRI (Urban Design Research Institute) in Mumbai completed an extensive study of the Fort Area of the city (Mehrotra and Nest, 1994). It has recently gone beyond the documentation phase to lead the conservation effort in the Kala Ghoda area (1998+) where some fine colonial-Gothic and other institutional and commercial buildings are located. The area, now the site of an annual arts festival, has been upgraded as the result of a program led by Rahul Mehrotra and Abha Narain Lambha with the contribution of institutions and individuals with a direct commitment to the area. Piece by piece, the companies involved have tidied up the precinct, improved the pavements and added amenities. The goal is to further upgrade the area by restoring the buildings. Similar efforts are now being made to establish a banking district around Horniman Circle and to upgrade the Ballard Estate (Mehrotra, 2000). The foreground to the Gateway of India, a politically

The Kamala Mills renovation [NRK House now], Mumbai

sensitive site, has been redesigned but the proposal to give some visual dignity to the area remains up in the air (Somaya, 2000). Proposals similar to these are in the works for other cities. In Udaipur, for example, the Ahmedabad group Abhikram is devising approaches for maintaining the quality of streets of vernacular buildings. The quality of streets, not simply buildings, is thus back on the designer's agenda after the Modernist hiatus.

The preservation and conservation efforts of the 1990s succeeded in saving a number of buildings that give cities a sense of time and place. These buildings enrich the life of all a city's inhabitants and act as part of the everyday educative environment of children and adults alike.

The Incipient Era of Information Technology

New architectures arise when changing structures of society present architects with opportunities to explore new lines of thought. Since the development of ENIAC, the first modern computer in the 1940s, and more particularly with the development of the Internet in the 1990s, pundits have speculated on the changes that will take places in societies around the world as a result of the information revolution. The changes have come much slower than predicted. It is, however, clear that changes in information technology will continue the process of 'globalising' the world begun during the period of European colonisation of Asia, Africa and the Americas.

Architecture itself has responded little to the new age at either the spatial or symbolic level. It will no doubt follow changes in ways of life instigated by information technology. New building types will emerge replacing some of the old; but day-to-day ways of life for the middle class are unlikely to change much during the next two generations. Certainly, a number of architects are aware that changes in urban form will occur and that working habits that depend on communication processes will change. Sen Kapadia, in his design for Sumeru Apartments, recognised that 'homes for the future are destined to be workplaces also'. He made the assumption that such a change will lead to people needing to meet each other more frequently on the local level. In the design of the complex, places for informal gatherings were included as part of the built form.

Such explorations are still rare. Certainly, we are aware that a number of the intuitively obvious assumptions that we have made about the impact of the new information technology on people's lives have proven to be, if not erroneous, hardly what we expected. What has arrived is the 'smart office' or 'intelligent building' in which, ideally, a system of energy efficiency, safety systems (fire control and personal security), a telecommunications frame and individual workplace requirements, including maximum automation, are integrated into a computer algorithm controlled whole.

The major effect of these demands on the design of buildings has, so far, been in the provision of concealed conduiting and false floors that allow for various cabling layouts. These elements have been included in a variety of buildings: the Bharat Diamond Bourse (1990+, but now standing unfinished) and Air Freight House, both in Mumbai, the FICCI (Federation of Indian Chambers of Commerce) Tower in Delhi and the Millennium Plaza (1999+) in nearby Gurgaon, for instance. These buildings have more of the personal imprint of their architects rather than any imprint of the new technology. Some architects in the future will no doubt wish to give new technological requirements an architectural expression.

A REFLECTION

The last three decades of the twentieth century saw the development of a variety of architectural practices working for a variety of clients. Superficially, the emerging efforts to deal with the modern world and create better futures may seem chaotic. They are not. What has become clear is that Modernist architectural ideas and principles are fine and work well in responding to specific problems. The host of wonderful Modernist buildings, custom-built houses in particular, attest to that. The limitations of Modernist thought are also clear, particularly in countries such as India, and particularly in establishing a sense of place anywhere. Buildings such as the Stock Exchange in Mumbai, fine though they may be, say little about locality. How to achieve a sense of place in an increasingly placeless world remains a challenge to architects.

The concern will be with the quality of life for all people on a much broader scale than the functionalists of modernism considered. Addressing the concern will require greater collaboration between professions. Such collaboration can only come with each profession being confident in its knowledge base and abilities, confident enough to recognise the limitations of that base as well as its breadth.

The bulk of India's design production is in the hands of the builder-contractor and will remain so in the foreseeable future. At the same time, there seem to be a number of directions in which architects are taking the country's architecture. Each responds to specific problems. In the future, some purist Modernist buildings will probably be built. There will certainly be a continuation of the Modern Indian Vernacular. Chronologically distinguishable referents will be used as various architectures of the past capture architects' and their clients' imaginations. Much commercial architecture will remain at the periphery of artistic and intellectual trends. Architects will pick up symbolic allusions to being up-to-date from new ideas in the fine and performing arts. A small body of work based on the assumption that architecture is indeed a pure fine art will continue to be built. It will be important in terms of the amount of attention it attracts but less so it terms of its impact on the profession's activities or on everyday life. What is being seen is a merging of Rationalist and Empiricist lines of thought. What has disappeared is the fear amongst architects of being automatically cast as non-creative when looking at what has and has not worked in the past, climatically, socially and aesthetically.

Perhaps the most significant continuing trend in architecture in India and its greatest potential contribution to thinking around the world is that the country's architects are looking into themselves to develop the divergent lines of thinking appropriate to them. At Independence, India thought of itself as something special, a country that would evolve into something unique. Much remains to be done to achieve this end. Architects will need to deal with new ways of life, new technologies and new construction methods; there is a need to seek new architectural ways even as the past remains with us. Like it or not, the ghost of Claude Batley along with those of Le Corbusier and Kahn haunt India. No doubt those of Correa, Doshi, Kanvinde and the host of others whose names parade through this book will come back to peer over the shoulders of future generations of architects too.

Glossary

affordance	The property of an object or environment that enables it to be used or interpreted in a specific range of ways.
Anglo-Indian	In this book, a British resident of India; nowadays, a Eurasian of colonial descent.
bas-relief	Carved work that projects less than half its true depth from its background.
brise-soleil	A latticed device used to block sunrays from entering a building.
beton brut	Concrete work in which the texture of the shuttering can be seen.
chhajjas	Dripstone, overhanging stone slab cornice, eave.
chhattri	Domed kiosk or small pavilion; often acting as a turret on a roof.
chowk	Courtyard, square.
civic baroque	The highly embellished form of classical architecture used for major municipal building complexes.
cubical form	One in which the height, width and depth of a building have roughly the same dimensions.
cupola	Small dome.
desert cooler	A low cost cooling device in which air is passed through a damp coir mat.
dharamsala	A rest house for Buddhist (or Hindu) pilgrims.
Dravidian	Historical style of South Indian architecture.
eave	Overhang sheltering a wall or porch.
embodied energy	The energy required to produce a product.
first floor	The floor just above the ground floor; not the ground floor.
garbha-griha	Inner sanctum of a temple.
haveli	Mansion with interior courtyard; wealthy merchant's house.
jaali	Lattice or filigree screen.
Kalibari	The temple of goddess Kali.

India faces many opportunities and problems. Architects, working as architects, can only address a small set of them. Probably the major ones have to do with the nature of human habitats, which increasingly means cities and city design.

The Stock Exchange [Share Market], Mumbai

lakh	1,00,000; One hundred thousand; 100,000.
lintel	A beam supporting a wall above an opening.
mandala	A geometric representation of the world.
mandapa	A hall or pillared pavilion. Congregational space.
mistri	A master craftsman; commonly, a carpenter.
mohalla	A traditional neighbourhood of a north Indian city.
Neo-Classical Architecture	Revivalist Greco-Roman architecture.
pediment	A moulding, or triangular form above an opening.
pilaster	Small column applied to a wall.
pilotes	Free-standing ground-floor columns supporting the first floor of a building.
plinth	Block or stone slab base for a statue, column or wall.
plotted houses	Houses built by the owners themselves on a site purchased by them.
pol	A territorially defined neighbourhood in the old cities of Gujarat and Rajasthan.
port cochere (portico)	A roofed structure extending from a building over a driveway to shelter people arriving at it.
shikhara	North Indian temple tower.
stucco	Plaster.
stupa	A bee-hive shaped Buddhist burial or reliquary mound.
square form	One in which the sides measure the same but not the height.
verandah	A roofed porch or balcony running along the side of a building.
zenana	Womens' living area in upper-class Muslim homes.

Bibliography

Ahuja, Sarayu (1998), 'Sen and Sensibility'. *Indian Architect & Builder* 11 (March): 32–52.

Alff, Jon (1991), 'Art Deco: Gateway to Indian Modernism'. *Architecture + Design* 8 (6): 57–63.

Ameen, Farooq, ed. (1997), *Contemporary Architecture and City Form: The South Asian Paradigm.* Mumbai: Marg Publications.

Architecture + Design 13 (2), 'Tribute: Habib Rahman'. Whole issue.

Bahga, Sarabjit, Surinder Bahga and Yashinder Bahga (1993). *Modern Architecture in India.* New Delhi: Galgotia Press.

——— (1997). *New Indian Homes: An Architectural Renaissance.* New Delhi: Galgotia.

Baker, Laurie (1990), 'The People and Architecture'. *Journal of the Indian Institute of Architects* 55 (1): 27–9.

Banerji, Geraldine S-P (1998), 'The Seventies'. *Inside-Outside* 155: 128–39.

Barry, John (1954). *Calcutta Illustrated* (second edition). Calcutta: Central Press.

Batley, Claude (1954), 'Indian Architecture Today'. *Journal of the Indian Institute of Architects* 20 (3): 11–12.

Bhatia, Gautam (1991), *Laurie Baker, Life, Work and Writings.* New Delhi: Penguin India.

——— (1994a), *Punjabi Baroque and Other Memories of Architecture.* New Delhi: Penguin, India.

——— (1994b), *Silent Spaces and Other Stories of Architecture.* New Delhi: Penguin India.

Bhatt, Vikram and Peter Scriver (1990), *Contemporary Indian Architecture: After the Masters.* Ahmedabad: Mapin.

Blake, Peter (1977), *Form Follows Fiasco: Why Modern Architecture Hasn't Worked.* Boston: Little Brown.

Brolin, Brent (1976), *The Failure of Modern Architecture.* New York: Van Nostrand Reinhold.

Brooks, H. Allen (1997), *Le Corbusier's Formative Years. Charles Edouard Jeanneret at La Chaux-de-Fondes.* Chicago: University of Chicago Press,

Bubbar, Darshan (forthcoming), *The Spirit of Indian Architecture.* Mumbai: BPI (India).

Chandavarkar, Prem (1989), 'Men's Hostel, Indian Institute of Science'. *Indian Architect and Builder* 2 (11): 13–14.

——— (1991), 'Towards a Natural Architecture'. *Architecture + Design* 4 (5): 94–9.

Chatterjee, Malay (1985), 'The Evolution of Contemporary Indian Architecture'. In Raj Rewal et al., eds, *Architecture in India.* Paris: Electa Moniteur: 124–72.

——— (1996), 'Habib Rahman and His Times'. *Architecture + Design* 13 (2), 'Tribute: Habib Rahman'. Whole issue.

Chatterjee, Sris Chandra (1942), *Magadha Architecture.* Calcutta: Calcutta University Press.

——— (1948), *The Architect and Architecture: Then and Now.* Calcutta: Calcutta University Press.

Chaudhry, Uttara (1989), 'The Spread and Acceptance of Architectural Images and Idioms: The Case Study of Ahmedabad'. Unpublished diploma dissertation, School of Architecture, CEPT, Ahmedabad.

Chauhan, Uttara (1998), 'Rites of Initiation'. *Architect and Builder* 11 (11): 22–7.

Correa, Charles (1984), 'The Assembly'. *The Architects' Journal* 179 (June): 32–9.

——— (1996), *Charles Correa.* Bombay: Perennial Press.

Curtis, William (1985), 'The Ancient in the Modern'. In Raj Rewal et al., eds. *Architecture in India.* Paris: Electa Moniteur: 81–90.

——— (1988), *Balkrishna Doshi: An Architect for India.* New York: Rizzoli.

Das, S.K. (1991), 'Enabling the Rural User'. *Architecture + Design* 8 (1): 50–1.

Desai, Madhavi (1998), 'Integration of Landscape with a Formal Design'. *Inside Outside* 155: 113–17.

Deshpandi, R. (1939 [1948]), *Modern Homes for India.* Revised Edition. Poona: United Book Corporation.

Devi, Gayatri, ed. (1999), *Vastu, Astrology and Architecture.* Delhi: Motilal Banarsidass Publishers.

Doctor, Geeta (1998), 'Recalling the Waves'. *Inside Outside* 155: 164–7.

Dormitory pour les adherents di Sri Aurobindo: Antonin Raymond, arch. (1951), *Architecture d'Anjourdhui* 22 (December): 68–70.

Doshi, Balkrishna V. (1996), Interview. *Architecture + Design* 13 (6). 58–62.

Dwivedi, Sharada and Rahul Mehrotra (1995), *Bombay: The Cities Within.* Bombay: The India Bookhouse.

Eames, Charles and Ray Eames (1967), 'The Eames Report 1958'. *Marg* 20, (3) (June): 22–8.

Eaton, Leonard (1969), *Two Chicago Architects and their Clients. Frank Lloyd Wright and Howard van Doren Shaw.* Cambridge, MA: MIT Press.

Editors, The (1989), 'Romi Khosla'. *Mimar* 30: 29–51.

Evenson, Norma (1966), *Chandigarh.* Berkeley and Los Angeles: University of California Press.

——— (1989), *The Indian Metropolis: The View Towards the West.* Delhi: Oxford University Press.

Fathy, Hassan (1969), *Architecture for the Poor.* Chicago: University of Chicago Press.

Fitch, James Marston (1960), *Walter Gropius.* London: Mayflower.

Frampton, Kenneth (1996), 'The Works of Charles Correa'. In Charles Correa (ed.), *Charles Correa.* Bombay: Perennial Press: 8–16.

——— (1997), 'The Predicament of the Place-form'. In Farooq Ameen, ed., *Contemporary Architecture and City Form: The South Asia Paradigm.* Mumbai: Marg Publications: 101–8.

G[randcolas], Alain (1992), *Auroville: A Dream Takes Shape.* Pondicherry: Sri Aurobindo Press.

Garnier, Tony (1917), 'Une Cité Industrielle: etude pour la construction de villes'. Paris: Auguste Vincente. Reprinted New York: Rizzoli, 1990.

Ghirardo, Diane (1996), *Architecture After Modernism.* London: Thames and Hudson.

Ghosh, Arnab (1998), 'Vernacular Architecture: A Study of Concerned Aspects and Its Reflection in Contemporary Indian Architecture'. Unpublished diploma dissertation, School of Architecture, CEPT, Ahmedabad.

Gropius, Walter (1962), *The Scope of Total Architecture.* New York: Collier.

Grover, Razia (1991), *Concepts and Responses: International Architectural Design Competition for the Indira Gandhi National Centre for the Arts.* Ahmedabad: Mapin.

Grover, Satish (1995), *Building Beyond Borders: Story of Contemporary Indian Architecture.* New Delhi: National Book Trust.

——— (1996), 'Interview'. *Architecture + Design.* 13 (6). 66–7.

Gujarat State PWD (undated), *Gandhinagar: New Capital of Gujarat.* Baroda: Government Press.

Gujral, Satish (1993). *The World of Satish Gujral in His Own Words.* New Delhi: UBSPD.

Gupta, Samita (1991), 'Sris Chandra Chatterjee: The Quest for a National Architecture'. *The Indian Economic and Social History Review.* 28 (2): 187–201.

Huet, Bernard (1987), 'Indira Gandhi National Centre'. *Mimar* (March): 37–9.

Iengar, Kheshavram N. (1994), *Education for Architecture: Programme for Concord.* Mysore: Academy of Art and Architecture.

——— (1996), *Composing Architecture.* Mysore: Academy of Art and Architecture.

Itten, Johannes (1965), 'The Foundation Course at the Bauhaus'. In Gyorgy Kepes, ed., *The Education of Vision.* New York: George Braziller: 104–21.

Jain, Uttam (1991), 'Modern Architecture in India'. *Journal of the Indian Institute of Architects* 37 (1): 17–20.

Joglekar, M.N. and S.K. Das (1995), *Contemporary Indian Architecture: Housing and Urban Development.* New Delhi: Galgotia.

Joshi, Kiran (1999), *Documenting Chandigarh: The Indian Architecture of Pierre Jeanneret, E. Maxwell Fry and Jane Drew.* Ahmedabad: Mapin.

Khanna, Anna (1998), 'A Design to Free the Body and Spirit'. *Inside Outside* 163: 166–72.

Kalia, Ravi (1987), *Chandigarh: In Search of an Identity.* Carbondale: Southern Illinois University Press.

——— (1994), *Bhubaneswar: From Temple Town to Capital City*. Delhi: Oxford University Press.

Khan, Hasan-Uddin (1987), *Charles Correa*. Singapore: Concept Media.

Khosla, Romi (1991), 'Current Architecture in India'. *Mimar* 41 (December): 20–5.

Kirkham, Pat (1995), *Charles and Ray Eames: Designers of the Twentieth Century*. Cambridge, MA: MIT Press.

Koenigsberger, Otto (1952), 'New Towns in India'. *Town Planning Review* 23 (2): 95–132.

Krishan, Arvind (2000), 'Climate Responsible Architecture'. Delhi: Tata McGraw Hill.

Kruty, Paul. (1998), 'Creating a Modern Architecture for India'. In Anne Watson, ed., *Beyond Architecture: Marion Mahony and Walter Burley Griffin—America Australia India*. Sydney. Powerhouse Museum: 138–59.

Kshirsagar, G.B. (1941), 'Revival of Indian Architecture?' *Journal of the Indian Institute of Architects* 7 (2): 89.

Lang, Jon (1987), *Creating Architectural Theory: The Role of the Behavioral Sciences in Environmental Design*. New York: Van Nostrand Reinhold.

——— Madhavi Desai and Miki Desai (1997), *Architecture and Independence: The Search for Identity—India 1880 to 1980*. Delhi: Oxford University Press.

Le Corbusier (1953), *The Marseilles Block*. Translated from the French by Geoffrey Sainsbury. London: Harvill.

——— (1954), *The Modulor*. Translated from the French by Peter de Francis and Anna Bostock: Cambridge, MA: MIT Press.

——— (1961), 'I. The Master Plan, II. The Capitol'. *Marg* 15 (1): 5–19.

——— (1963), *My Work*. Translated from the French by James Palmer. London: Architectural Press.

Lohana, Jyotsna (1998), 'A Maverick Architect'. *Indian Architect and Builder* 12 (November): 32–8.

M.A.R.G. (1947), 'Creative Architecture or Regressive Revivalism'? *Journal of the Indian Institute of Architects* 15 (4): 77.

Mayer, Albert (1950), 'New Capital of Punjab'. *American Institute of Architects' Journal* 14 (4): 166–75.

McManus, Peter (1993), 'The Polish Connection'. *Swagat* (November): 12–19.

Mehrotra, Rahul and Gunter Nest (1994), *The Fort Precinct in Bombay: Conserving an Image Centre*. Bombay: Urban Design Research Institute.

Meller, Helen E. (1977), 'Patrick Geddes and His Contribution to the Modern Town Planning Movement in Pre-independent India'. *Urban and Regional Planning Thought* 20 (January–March): 1–7.

Menon, A.G. Khrishna (1990), 'The Architecture of Religious Buildings'. *Architecture + Design* 7 (1): 87–99.

Mhatre, Gajanan B. (1937), 'Flats on Backbay Reclamation'. *Journal of the Indian Institute of Architects* 3 (3): 270–1.

Michell, George and Antonio Martinelli (1994), *The Royal Palaces of India.* London: Thames and Hudson.

Mitter, Partha (1994), *Art and Nationalism in Colonial India, 1850–1922.* Cambridge: Cambridge University Press.

Mohandas, S.K. (1988), 'Ganeshnagar: A Settlement Improvement Programme'. *Architecture + Design* 4 (2): 26–9.

Mumford, Lewis (1954), 'Nowicki's Work in India'. *Architectural Record* 116 (3): 153–9.

Nilsson, Sten Ake (1973), *The New Capitals of India, Pakistan and Bangladesh.* London: Curzon Press.

Oza, Nilay (1995), 'National Histories and Architectural Patronage'. Unpublished diploma dissertation, School of Architecture, CEPT, Ahmedabad.

Pallasmaa, Juhani (1988), 'Tradition and Modernity: The Feasibility of Regional Architecture in Post-modern Society'. *Architectural Review* 183 (1095): 27–34.

Panchal, Kunjal (1998), 'The Architecture of Achyut Kanvinde: A Study of Houses in Ahmedabad'. Unpublished diploma dissertation, School of Architecture, CEPT, Ahmedabad.

Pandya, Yatin (1993), 'A Disciplined Minimalist'. *Architecture + Design* 10 (3). 30–5.

Paradkar, Shalaka (1998), 'A Democratic Brio'. *Indian Architect and Builder* 11 (March): 52–66.

Parwani-Talib, Kavita (1999), 'Assertive Interpretation'. *Indian Architect and Builder* 13 (2). 45–55.

Pereira José (1995), *Baroque Goa.* New Delhi: Books and Books.

Pica, Agnoldomenico (1979), 'Eckart Muthesius in India, 1930–4: The Avant-garde Meets History'. *Domus* 593: 1–11.

Prasad, Sunand (1987), 'Le Corbusier in India'. *Architecture + Design* 3 (6): 14–27.

Prakash, Sanjay (1986), 'The Structured Poetry of Mahendra Raj'. *Architecture + Design* 3 (1): 15–33.

——— (1989), 'Change, Participation and Process: A Road Map'. *Architecture + Design* 8 (1): 18–22.

Prakash, Vikramaditya (1999), *Chandigarh: The City Beautiful.* Chandigarh: Abhisek Publishers.

Prithi, Anupam (1991), 'Designing with Freedom'. *Inside Outside* 82: 98–120.

Rapoport, Amos (1977), *Human Aspects of Urban Design.* New York: Pergamon.

Raulet, Sylvia (1996), *Maharajas' Palaces.* Paris: Editions Hazan.

Raymond, Antonin (1973), *An Autobiography.* Rutland, Vermont: Charles E. Tuttle Company.

Raza, Mohmad H. (1953), 'The Osmania University Project'. *Journal of the Indian Institute of Architects* 19 (4): 7–12.

Rewal, Raj (1986), *Raj Rewal.* Milan: Electa Moniteur.

Rudofsky, Bernard (1964), *Architecture without Architects.* New York: Museum of Modern Art.

Sert, José Luis and C.I.A.M (1944), *Can our Cities Survive? An ABC of Urban Problems, Their Analysis and Solutions.* Cambridge, MA: Harvard University Press.

Shah, Jagan (1992), 'Satish Grover: A Sense of History'. *Architecture + Design* 9 (4): 19–44.

Shah, Kirtee (1988), 'Vasna: A Decade Later'. *Architecture + Design* 4 (2): 74–7.

Shah, Ranvir (1997), 'Signature Domes, Pyramids and Triangles'. *Inside Outside* 150 (October): 76–92.

Smith, G.E. Kidder (1950), *Sweden Builds.* London: Architectural Press.

Spence, Robin (1980), 'Laurie Baker: Architect for the Indian Poor'. *Architectural Association Quarterly* 12 (1): 30–9.

Steele, James (1998), *The Complete Architecture of Balkrishna Doshi: Rethinking Modernism for the Developing World.* London: Thames and Hudson.

Tafel, Edgar (1945), 'India's Largest Architectural Firm'. *Architectural Forum* 82 (5): 58.

Taylor, Brian Brace (1991), 'SCOPE City Citadel'. *Mimar.* 13: 16–25.

——— (1992), *Raj Rewal.* London: Mimar Publications and Concept Media.

Thapar, Romila (1992), 'Tradition and Change'. In B.B. Taylor, *Raj Rewal,* op cit., 19–24.

Tillotson, Giles H. (1989), *The Tradition of Indian Architecture: Continuity, Controversy and Change Since 1850.* New Haven: Yale University Press.

Tschumi, Bernard (1988), 'Notes Towards a Theory of Architectural Disjunction'. *Architecture and Urbanism* 216: 11–15.

Vaz, Julius L.K. (1954), 'Architecture of Bhubaneswar, New Capital, Orissa'. *Journal of the Indian Institute of Architecture* 15 (2): 3–4.

Venturi, Robert (1966), *Complexity and Contradiction in Modern Architecture.*New York: Museum of Modern Art.

Weirick, James (1981), *The Magic of America: Vision and Text.* In Jenepher Duncan and Merryn Gates, eds, *Walter Burley Griffin—A Review.* Clayton, VIC: Monash University Gallery: 5–14.

White, Stephen (1993), *Building in the Garden: The Architecture of Joseph Allen Stein in India and California.* Delhi: Oxford University Press.

Williamson, Roxanne (1991), *American Architects and the Mechanics of Fame.* Austin, TX: University of Texas Press.

Wingler, Hans (1969), *The Bauhaus: Weimar, Dessau, Berlin, Chicago.* Translated from the German by Wolfgang Jabs and Basil Gilbert, edited by Joseph Stein. Cambridge, MA: MIT Press.

Wolfe, Tom (1981), *From Bauhaus to Our House.* New York: Farrar, Strauss, Giroux.

Yeang, Ken (1996), *The Skyscraper Bioclimatically Considered: A Design Primer.* London: Academy Editions.

Interviews and Personal Communications Cited

Benninger, Christopher (2000), Architect, Pune.

Bhoosan, Dr B.S. (2000), Architect, Mysore.

Correa, Charles (2000), Architect, Mumbai

Dadkar, Akhil (1996), Architect, Mumbai.

Dalal, Abhimanyu (2000), Architect, New Delhi.

Devane, Andrew (1996), Architect, Dublin, Ireland. An apprentice at Taliesen, Scotsdale, Arizona, USA (1944–6).

Doshi, B.V. (1988), Architect and educator, Ahmedabad.

Kanvinde, Achyut (2000), Architect, New Delhi.

Lerner, Ralph (2000), Architect and educator, Princeton, New Jersey, USA.

Majumdar, Dipak (2000), Architect, Calcutta.

Mehrotra, Rahul J. (1999, 2000), Architect and urban designer, Mumbai.

Patel, Dr Bimal (1999), Architect, Ahmedabad.

Patel, Nimish (2000), Architect and urban designer, Ahmedabad.

Pithavadian, Bennett (1984,1988), Architect, Chennai.

Rahman, Habib (1988,1994), Architect, New Delhi.

Rao, Kavita Daryani (2000), Architect and educator, Hyderabad.

Acknowledgments

THIS BOOK draws heavily on the research carried out for a prior work—*Architecture and Independence: The Search for Identity—India: 1880 to 1980.* Without the collaboration of Madhavi Desai and Miki Desai that study would never have been contemplated, let alone completed. The list of people who made a substantive contribution to that volume is lengthy and they will see that their contribution to it carried forward here. I am especially grateful to the Desais for their continued support and for allowing me free rein with their material in assembling this book. They are not listed as co-authors simply because they cannot be held responsible for the interpretations within it.

This book is, however, no mere clone of that earlier endeavour. Year by year, architectural scholarship in India yields greater insights into the nature of the discipline and its artefacts. Buildings not covered in that earlier work have been introduced here and this work has given me an opportunity to clarify a number of topics dealt with in the earlier book.

Like its predecessor, this volume is based on the studies of many Indian architects, academics and an extraordinary array of students in and of the field. It is also based on a broad range of interviews and much fieldwork. Conducting interviews, documenting buildings and processing photographs is expensive. Without the original support of the Australian Research Council from 1993 to 1996 and again in 2000, and from the Faculty of the Built Environment at the University of New South Wales in 1999, it would have been impossible for this study to have been completed. Many other organisations and individuals have unselfishly contributed their time and energy to making this endeavour financially viable.

There are a number of individuals who have made specific contributions to this work who should be singled out. The substantive contribution of the Desais in Ahmedabad has already been noted. A large number of other people have helped me try to 'get things right'. They include Christopher Benninger, Sherish Beri, Sonali Bhagwati, Gautam Bhatia, B.S. Bhooshan, Darshan Bubbar, Prem and

Nina Chandavarkar, Akhtar Chauhan, S.L. Chitale, Hafeez Contractor, Charles Correa, Akhil Dadkar, Geeta Doctor, Abhimanyu Dalal, Ujan Ghosh, Satish Grover, Achyut Kanvinde, Sen Kapadia, Ralph Lerner, Dipak Majumdar, Rahul Mehrotra, Vergis Oommen, Bimal Patel, Nimish Patel, Anant Raje, K. Rajagopalan, Kavita Daryani-Rao, Anand Shirgaokar, Brinda Somaya, Hemu Upadhyay, and Sarita Vijayan. The knowledge I gained in teaching with B.V. Doshi during the 1980s was the launching pad for this endeavour. I am particularly indebted to those who read this book, or parts of it, in manuscript form and offered advice on how it could be improved: Srikanth Adijopula, Madhavi Desai, Miki Desai, Harshad Bhatia, Geeta Doctor, Dr Peter Kohane, and Kashyap Rangan. Not least of the individuals whom I have to thank is Anuradha Roy. It was her original suggestion that initiated this particular endeavour and it has been she who has seen it home.

CREDITS

The sources of all the material used in this book are cited in the text. Other than those listed below, I am the copyright-holder of all the photographs and illustrations used in this text or they are in the public domain. The line drawings are the work of Kashyap Rangan. In assembling the other illustrations I have been helped by an extraordinarily generous group of individuals and I am grateful for their permission to use their work. Christopher Benninger, Sherish Beri, Harshad Bhatia, Dhansukh Bhatt, B.S. Bhoosan, Charles Correa, Achyut Kanvinde, K.S. Ranganath, Anant Raje, A.M. Shirgaokar, Brinda Somaya and Upalghosh Associates all allowed me to use their own photographs of their work. Miki Desai provided the photographs of Golconde in Pondicherry, the LIC Building in Chennai and St John's Cathedral in Tiruvella, and Leo Perreria the photographs of his house taken by Dinesh Mehta. John Glew sent me the photograph of the Aga Khan award winning Leper's Hospital. Rahul Mehrotra provided the photograph of his office taken by Rajesh Vora. The photograph of the Fagus factory was a part of Walter Gropius's own collection. The Frank Lloyd Wright Foundation in Scottsdale, Arizona holds the copyright of the drawing of the Calico Mills project and the Avery Library at Columbia University that of Burley Griffin's design for the Ahmedabad Town Hall. The photograph of the United States Embassy in New Delhi is published courtesy of Public Affairs, the American Embassy. Vikram Bhatt and Peter Scriver allowed me to use photographs of the Modern School in Vasant Vihar and the Dudhsagar Dairy Complex taken from their book *After the Masters.* I thank them all.

Drawing on many sources, despite my best intentions, errors are likely to have occurred in this book. Every effort has been made to corroborate data and to contact and credit copyright holders of all the illustrations used. Errors of commission should be brought to my attention at the Faculty of the Built Environment, University of New South Wales, Sydney 2052, Australia. Others will have to respond to errors of omission.

Index